Political thought and public policy in the nineteenth century

POLITICAL THOUGHT AND PUBLIC POLICY IN THE NINETEENTH CENTURY

An introduction

Robert Pearson
and Geraint Williams

LONGMAN
London and New York

LONGMAN GROUP LIMITED
Longman House, Burnt Mill, Harlow
Essex CM20 2JE, England
Associated companies throughout the world

*Published in the United States of America
by Longman Inc., New York*

© Longman Group Limited 1984

First published 1984

BRITISH LIBRARY CATALOGUING IN PUBLICATION DATA
Pearson, Robert.
    Political thought and public policy in the
    nineteenth century.
    1. Great Britain – Politics and government – 1800–1837
    2. Great Britain – Politics and government – 1837–1901
    I. Title   II. Williams, Geraint
    320.941   DA535

    ISBN 0-582-29595-5

LIBRARY OF CONGRESS CATALOGING IN PUBLICATION DATA
Pearson, Robert.
    Political thought and public policy in the
nineteenth century.

    Bibliography: p.
    Includes index.
    1. Political science – Great Britain – History – 19th
century.   2. Great Britain – Politics and government –
19th century.   I. Williams, Geraint,   1942–
II. Title.
JA84.G7P4   1984   320.5′0941   83-1150
ISBN 0-582-29595-5

Set in 10/11 pt Linotron 202 Plantin
Printed in Hong Kong
by Astros Printing Limited

CONTENTS

PREFACE

Our intention in writing this book is to bring together the study of history and the study of political thought. Both are too often studied in isolation so that political ideas and political history become two separate areas of enquiry. While a great number of students study the history of the nineteenth century and also its political thought there are few books written which seek to integrate the two activities. We believe that the most fruitful way of approaching this period is to see it in terms of the relationship between political theory and political practice.

Although a great deal of the political debate of this period took place in journals, we have as far as possible referred to the more accessible books in order that the reader can more easily check or dispute our interpretations. For those who wish to go deeper into the ideas and the history of the century, and more importantly into the debate about the sources of reform in this period, we have included a bibliography which we hope will act as a guide to the main modern controversies as well as to the nineteenth-century material, the journals as well as the books.

In presenting our attempt to do this we have drawn on our experience in teaching at the University of Sheffield and the Sheffield City Polytechnic. We are also grateful to those two institutions for granting us the necessary study leave in which to write this book; our thanks also to the University of Sheffield Research Fund for financial help.

Our main thanks, of both an intellectual and a practical nature, go to Professor Bernard Crick. His own refusal to accept the division between 'theory' and 'institutions', as well as his encouragement and advice in this venture, has been of immense help to us. We hope that the book is a tribute to his approach to the study of politics; its weaknesses, of course, are ours. Lastly, we are most grateful for the care with which Miss Lesley Fixman corrected and typed the manuscript.

Robert Pearson
Geraint Williams

INTRODUCTION

The aim of this book is to discuss the relationship between political theory and political practice in the nineteenth century. Putting it this way may give the impression that these are two separate activities, that practice can proceed without theory. The reality, however, is that political activity could not begin to be understood without the existence of concepts, ideas, and principles, however well hidden. If theory is often studied separately it is because its task is to articulate those assumptions which lie behind practical activity; similarly the study of practice is often isolated from theory. This work attempts to respect and reflect the intimate link between ideas and action.

Political action, to be rightly understood, involves ideas but here a distinction must be made between the ideas which define the activity and determine our view of the world, and those ideas which give us our aims, those values which we strive to fulfil. Thus in looking at the role of ideas in politics we must look at both those ideas which are intrinsic to the activity and those which influence the direction the activity takes. An example may help here: to understand the distinction between murder, manslaughter, suicide and abortion involves us in appreciating a whole range of moral ideas which make those activities what they are. The 'fact' of death is insufficient to describe the events. On this level ideas are necessary for a full description, but over and above this there are other ideas too which influence action, those for example justifying or condemning suicide, murder or abortion. Now some of these ideas may challenge the distinctions by which others see the world, but disputes can take place over the merits or demerits of suicide without changing the distinction between it and, say, murder. So in politics we must distinguish between the concepts which make the world intelligible and the principles which give it purpose and direction – it is the ignoring of this distinction which has led some writers to move from scepticism about the role of principles and values in politics to hostility to the role of ideas in general in politic al practice. Even if principles in politics could be dispensed with ideas would still play a crucial part in determining our view of wha is relevant, what is a problem and what is worthy of attention Thus, if we see certain economic laws as natural we shall not see them as subject to political action, and if we see men as naturally unequal we shall not aim at an egalitarian society. The ideas which inform our world affect our principles: it is easier to adopt a pater nalistic role for government if we hold a view of society as organic and hierarchical with a natural ruling élite than if we see it as a collection of individuals striving for self-interest.

In this book we shall try and convey both the ideas which char acterised the different political movements and those which gave them their purposes. We shall see that although there are links be tween these two sets of ideas there are also variations in the specific purposes put forward from people who share the same ideas about the nature of the political world.

If we can accept that ideas are intrinsic to political activity in the sense that action cannot be understood without ideas, what role can we expect of those principles and values often seen as motivators or guides to political action? Do the principles put forward by political thinkers affect the conduct of practitioners? Does theory influence behaviour over and above those ideas necessary to understand the behaviour at all? Clearly a Marxist and a Utilitarian will disagree on their descriptions of what are the key elements in politics, but what sort of impact do we expect their general princi ples to have on their practice? Are ideas the crucial factor in deter mining events or simply a rationalisation or summary of existing behaviour? Before we answer, let us look for a moment at the possible role of general principles in political life. There is a sense in which it is odd to look for any close logical connection – at least of a deductive sort – between general theory and specific action, or programmes of action, if only because there are always alternative causes of action consistent with the general theory. Thus, in the nineteenth century, the doctrines put forward by, say, liberalism and conservatism changed through time even though there were general principles which remained constant. Although there is a relationship between general theory and specific action, from the outside this looks like one of consistency rather than deduction. However, if we consider this from the inside, so to speak, the connection may be more intimate than logic would suggest. Thus the general principles may, for the actors involved, be necessary to their specific behaviour even though other behaviour would be equally consistent with them. If men's beliefs are necessary to an understanding of their actions, they are necessary whether or not they lead logically to such action. Furthermore, even if action is only consistent with theory rather than deduced logically from it, this in itself limits and affects such action. Thus a liberal or conservative perspective may not indicate only one possible course of action, but nevertheless it will limit the possibilities of action such that it matters which perspective is adopted. Which theory is held determines the view taken of the current traditions of behaviour in society, and the support or challenge to such traditions helps define what is seen as tolerable or intolerable, possible or impossible.

Of course ideas, in the sense of general theory or principles, are not the only aspect which influences behaviour in a particular situation. Economic interests, class conflicts, power relationships, all play a part (though even here these are largely unintelligible without attention to ideas about reality). While ideas cannot be neglected in the study of history – both ideas as concepts and ideas as values – the actual impact and influence of such ideas can only be assessed as the result of particular enquiry into a particular period. In writing this book we are clearly committed to a view of the importance of ideas – and in one sense at least, that of the necessity of seeing behaviour as ideas in action, we consider this beyond dispute. In the other sense, the impact of ideas on action, we must delay final judgement until the period under review has been considered more fully. It seems at this stage unlikely either that political principles counted for everything or that they counted for nothing; when we have looked at the ideas and changes in public policy we can assess their relative importance.

More specifically, we shall look at each of the five main bodies of ideas in the nineteenth century – utilitarianism, liberalism, conservatism, socialism and new liberalism. In addition we shall look at the main changes that took place in public policy – those political, social, economic and administrative changes that took place as the result of government action and which (as deliberate human action) could prima facie be considered as the result of changing ideas. The book will provide an account of the development of political thought and of public policy with the main interest being the exploration of the links between the two. The starting point for such a study is A. V. Dicey's classic work *The Relation Between Law and Public Opinion in England During the Nineteenth Century*. Although this has been much criticised it remains a fine exploration of the period. It has suffered to some extent because of the stereotypes, which Dicey appeared to apply to the century, expressed in his division between Individualism and Collectivism. Although he himself modified such a crude classification, and although his writing is sensitive and subtle on the changes which took place, he has often been condemned because of his headlines rather than his actual reportage. Thus while he did see a change from Individualism to Collectivism as the century progressed, he was also aware of the counter-currents and cross-currents existing simultaneously, and of the seeds of collectivism already present in the earlier period. His classification is over-simple but his qualifications to it have too often been ignored by his critics. Dicey contrasted a period from 1825 to 1867, that of Benthamism or Individualism, which he saw as attacking restrictions on individuals, with the period after 1867 which he saw as Collectivism, the growth of government activity. Within this contrast Dicey was well aware of the existence of conflicting tendencies. However, the case has been made that such forces – collectivist in the period of Individualism, and individualist in the period of Collectivism – were of such importance that the labels themselves must be seriously questioned. Thus, for example, state intervention and the growth of government agencies were crucial from 1832 on, thus challenging the description of this period as Individualist. Some critics have gone even further and attacked Dicey's claim that the main changes in legislative tendency were due to changes in opinion; they are especially sceptical of the influence he attributes to Bentham and his disciples in the earlier period. Whether Bentham's influence justified the individualist or the collectivist tendency is one question; whether the influence mattered at all is another. Perhaps changes in the direction of government policy were due to industrialisation, urbanisation and other social changes, and not to new ideas? To answer such questions we must assess the ideas put forward – the nature of Benthamism, its practical proposals – as well as evaluating its impact on changes in public policy. In each of the chapters we shall make a threefold division between the theory to be considered, the response of the theory to the existing state of society, and the changes in policy and how far they were due to the influence of ideas and how far to other factors. It may seem somewhat artificial to separate theory from practice in this way but we believe that the best way to attain the eventual integration of the whole is by first seeing the parts clearly. In order to gain a clear overall view of the century we have made the distinction between political theory, practical proposals and legislative impact, though we would not want to regard these as separate except for reasons of clarity. If at times the distinctions become blurred it is because the reality of integration always impinges on the making of such distinctions, however useful this may be on the road to understanding.

How do we account for the changes which undoubtedly did take place in the nineteenth century? When we have considered the developments in ideas and policy and the relationship between them we shall attempt an answer. What looks clear at this stage is that whatever the force of economic or social conditions there were always alternative paths to pursue, and that the particular paths chosen owed a great deal to rival views of the world and of how to maintain or change it. Nothing can proceed without ideas; this is not to say that ideas alone determine all action. In looking at the influence of ideas we must not, of course, expect any crude and simple connection with practice. There may have been a few political actors – politicians and administrators – who studied the theory and attempted its implementation, but generally the ideas of political theorists operate in a less obvious way by influencing the assumptions and prejudices of political actors. That such practitioners of the business of politics may be unable to connect such assumptions to the ideas of particular theorists does not indicate the weakness of such a link but rather the complexity of the process by which ideas are disseminated. One can be influenced by a Darwin, a Marx, a Freud or a Bentham without having read their work. So, for the nineteenth century: that action was not always a conscious attempt to implement ideas does not mean the absence of influence, but rather that the language and values of politics can often be used regardless of their origins even though their meaning owes much to such origins.

If we turn now to the century itself, we see politics dominated at the beginning of the period by Whigs and Tories and at the end by Liberals and Conservatives; indeed, a part of this book is the story of the growth of these two modern political parties. Who and what were the Whigs and Tories? The Whigs claimed ancestry from those aristocratic rebels in the seventeenth century who had defended parliament, the law, their property and the Church of England against the claims of absolute monarchy. The limitation of monarchical power and the supremacy of parliament were claimed as Whig creations. By the late eighteenth century it was the party of aristocratic power, held together by its memory and its family connections rather than by any ideological unity. But it did share many beliefs, combining resistance to arbitrary or absolute power with support for the privilege and property of the landed élite; so that while some political change, if moderate, was acceptable, anything like social revolution was not. Their early defence of the subject's right to life, liberty and property against the unlimited rights of the Crown was, by the nineteenth century, replaced by a desire for order and stability under their own government. The Whig belief in their right to rule almost destroyed their old anti-authoritarian element. By tradition if not in reality there was nevertheless a 'liberal' element in Whiggery, and its future in the nineteenth century was to be in alliance with the Liberals until the party split in 1886 over Irish Home Rule, with the Whigs joining the Conservatives.

The Tories, similarly, traced their ancestry back to the seventeenth century as upholders of Church and State through the absolute authority of the Crown. Only a supreme monarchy acting through divine right could protect property and privilege; absolutism was the key to order and security. The Glorious Revolution of 1688, in which James II was removed and William and Mary were placed on the throne, clearly seriously questioned the continuance of this belief in absolutism and divine right. To maintain this belief would have meant rebellion against the new monarchy; to abandon it would leave little that was unlike Whiggery. What eventually occurred was the relocation of absolute sovereignty, divinely ordained, from the monarchy to the whole legislature of King, Lords and Commons. Authority could be preserved and order maintained against the Whig belief in limited government by consent. The Crown still held a high position and obedience was still demanded, in contrast to the Whig view of opposition to the Crown and the right of resistance. Both agreed that political participation rested on property, and in most cases this meant landed property; both also agreed on the importance of the Church of England, though here the Tories were less inclined to tolerate Dissenters than were the Whigs. By the beginning of the nineteenth century the Tories saw themselves as upholders of the constitution against the forces of radicalism and reform. Property, patronage, privilege and influence were the proper ingredients for maintaining the balanced mixture of the constitution. Liberty and order could only be maintained if the balance were preserved; thus reform, which meant strengthening the democratic element, must be resisted. The beauty of the political balance was that it reflected the social and economic structure: property was dominant in the latter and so it should be in the former. This was the Tory case against reform. The Whigs, too, accepted the supreme role of property but were more open to the claims of new forms of property arising from the development of industry and commerce. They were also aware of the need to learn from the lesson of the French Revolution of 1789 – that moderate reform might be necessary to prevent violent revolution. Thus the Whigs, while resisting radical demands for parliamentary reform as a means to wider political and social reforms, nevertheless accepted that some preventative reforms must be countenanced.

As it was, the extension of the franchise and the redistribution of seats was a slow process – the first Reform Act of 1832 was a very moderate affair; then came Acts in 1867, 1884 and 1918. The first Act was passed by a Whig ministry, the second by Conservatives, the third and fourth by Liberals. How these came about we shall consider in the relevant sections, but the mere history of them and the administrations which passed them should warn us against any easy identification of Conservative with reactionary or Liberal with progressive: the history of parties in the nineteenth century is more complex than that. Furthermore, we should be aware that political parties at this time were not like their twentieth-century counterparts. Until the latter part of the century there were no national organisations mobilizing mass support; the parties were essentially parliamentary and even within that context lacked ideological unity: they were rather coalitions of different interests and different views. At different times throughout the century the Liberals represented an alliance between Whigs, Radicals, nonconformists, Free Traders and working-class representatives; the Conservatives similarly at different times included traditional Tories, paternalist philanthropists and industrialists.

In both camps at different times were those against intervention in social affairs and those in favour, those for the Empire and those against, for parliamentary reform and against, for Free Trade and against. In the country too they drew their support from different sections of the community at different times. Party ideology, unity and support were very varying phenomena throughout the century; often the strongest bond was hostility to the opposition. From 1830 to the end of the century, Whig-dominated alliances ruled for some twenty-two years. Liberal governments (taking 1859 as the 'beginning' of the Liberal party, when Whigs, Peelites and Radicals reached some sort of agreement to act together) for some twenty-one years, and Conservative administrations, including those of Peel before the split in the party and those of Derby, Disraeli and Salisbury after it, for some twenty-eight years. What changes occurred in the parties during this time, and what changes occurred in the country during their periods in office? How did they respond to the political, social and economic problems which faced Britain in this period? How far did their ideas on politics enable them to deal with problems and how far did they obstruct such a task? These are some of the questions we shall raise in tracing Britain's movement from an industrialising nation emerging victorious from the Napoleonic wars, through a period of world dominance and imperial expansion, to the beginning of the decline with the First World War. Within this context Britain was developing new institutions, political and administrative; the role of government in society and the economy was changing; the involvement and demands of different classes were likewise changing. The aim of this book is to look at some of those developments in the light of the ideas and principles which men brought to bear on their surroundings.

Chapter one
UTILITARIANISM

POLITICAL THEORY

Utilitarianism was a philosophy which flourished in England in the first half of the nineteenth century and, though it existed before that and its effect lasted long after, its main impact came through the writings of Jeremy Bentham and James Mill, and in a much modified way through the work of J. S. Mill. Before examining the version put forward by Bentham, it is important to see him both as a continuation of a previous tradition of thought and as someone reinforcing that tradition in response to what he saw as the dangerous dominance of custom.

The earlier exponent of utilitarianism had been David Hume (1711–1776), though his analysis of utility was not as precise as Bentham's, nor his application as detailed. Hume denied the traditional picture of man as being divided between reason and passion and argued that reason, far from opposing the passions, is controlled by them. Its aim is to serve: to secure those ends which the feelings approve of or what is called virtuous behaviour. What we call virtuous is what is useful to mankind, and the general rules and institutions of society exist because they are useful and thus gain general approval, and what gains approval is pleasure or some means to it. These three ideas – utility, virtue and pleasure – were the primary ideas which Bentham was to examine and use not as a conservative explanation of what exists but as a justification for attacking social rules and traditional institutions. Where Hume had argued that government, rules of justice and tradition could be shown to be useful to mankind, later utilitarians took the concept of usefulness and used it as a critical standard by which to judge government, rules of justice and traditional behaviour.

However, Bentham did not simply continue a tradition already in existence; he must also be seen in reaction to contemporary orthodoxy for he was essentially a practical thinker concerned not simply with the development of theory but with detailed reform. Bentham was born in the middle of the eighteenth century when the dominant ideas reflected the superiority of the aristocracy and the landed class. The latter part of the century was a period of ruling-class optimism before the French Revolution and reaction after it. While social abuse, suffering, poverty and crime were prevalent and radicalism increasing, the Tory orthodoxy was a glorification of the constitution and administration. In Bentham's hands utilitarianism became a weapon with which to challenge the establishment, thus converting a tradition of thought into an attack on the established order previously thought to be compatible with it. By applying utilitarian principles to a vast variety of political, legal, social and administrative problems he turned it from a moral theory to a reforming creed. He aimed to replace confusion, fiction and reaction with clarity, truth and progress, both in theoretical analysis and in practical reform.

Jeremy Bentham lived from 1748 to 1832, and having discovered the principle of utility early in his life he spent the rest of it exploring and applying the principle to a vast area of philosophical and social studies, gathering round him a group of able and dedicated followers. He was eager not only to establish a general formula for the happiness of the community but to discover a method by which to apply this to the detail of reform, and his disciples were experts in economics, law, politics and administration. In addition to those who might be called disciples, Bentham's circle of friends and admirers included many who held or were to hold positions of great prominence in the political, administrative, legal and literary life of the country. Sir Samuel Romilly had been Solicitor-General, Lord Brougham was to become Lord Chancellor; Edwin Chadwick and Southwood Smith became leading administrators; John and Edward Romilly, George Grote, Sir William Molesworth, Arthur Roebuck, Charles Buller were all to become members of parliament; others were contributors to or editors of some of the most influential newspapers and journals of the day. It was the most striking example in the nineteenth century of a group of intellectuals active in politics, of the attempt to link theory with practice.

Bentham's first published work, the *Fragment on Government*, appeared in 1776 and it exhibited the main characteristics of Benthamite writing – severe criticism of the opposition combined with proposals for reform based on the principle of utility. In this work he expresses his belief that 'it is the greatest happiness of the greatest number that is the measure of right and wrong',[1] and he uses this as the basis for criticising both current legal practice and current legal theory. He believed that with a clear first principle politics and law need no longer be full of inconsistency, obscurity, prejudice and confusion. Let us see exactly what Bentham's principle consisted of and on what psychological and moral views it was based. In his *Introduction to the Principles of Morals and Legislation* he expresses his fundamental position:

> Nature has placed mankind under the governance of two sovereign masters, *pain* and *pleasure*. It is for them alone to point out what we ought to do, as well as to determine what we shall do. On the one hand the standard of right and wrong, on the other the chain of causes and effects, are fastened to their throne.[2]

> By the principle of utility is meant that principle which approves or disapproves of every action whatsoever, according to the tendency which it appears to have to augment or diminish the happiness of the party whose interest is in question.[3]

Let us examine these two statements more closely. First, we see that for Bentham the cause of all actions, or for human actions what is called the motive, is always the pursuit of pleasure and the avoidance of pain. Psychologically or naturally, man can do no other. However, we need to distinguish here between psychological hedonism – that all human action is determined by pleasure and pain – and psychological egoism – that the pleasure and pain is always one's own. It is certainly clear that Bentham does believe that all values, purposes and goals are reducible to the desire for pleasure and the aversion to pain. This does not necessarily mean that his hedonism is egoistic, and indeed Bentham includes amongst his list of human motives good will or sympathy, benevolence, philanthropy, brotherly love, humanity, charity, pity, compassion and such motives. However, even if Bentham's hedonism, or his belief that pleasure is the basis of human action, is not necessarily egoistic or self-centred, nevertheless his view seems to be that generally 'self-preference' dominates all other considerations: although he never discounts altogether the social affections, his account of human motivation is one which stresses the self-regarding interests of man. In 1790 he refers to 'the universal, necessary and undisputed, and not even to be lamented property in human nature, the predominance of the self-regarding affections over the social'[4] and in 1830 he maintains that ordinarily 'self is everything, to which all other persons added to all other things put together, are as nothing'.[5]

If we move on a little we see that Bentham is saying more than that pleasure is the sole motive; he is also saying that pleasure alone is good. Indeed he uses the terms pleasure, happiness, useful and good almost interchangeably. He seems to be saying that what we mean by 'good' is that which gives pleasure. All pleasures are good, all pains are evil, therefore pleasure cannot be evaluated or criticised as such unless it is unwise; in other words only if it leads to more pain or denies a greater pleasure. It cannot on other grounds be morally wrong, as it is itself the basis of moral goodness. Goodness is now analysed in terms of pleasure and pain, and for this purpose Bentham assumes that all pleasures and pains are basically of a single logical type, In other words he does not consider whether toothache and remorse, hunger and sadness, are sufficiently similar to be compared as pains, or whether pushpin and poetry, the pleasures of the palate and friendship, are sufficiently similar to be compared as pleasure. The reason for his neglect of this part of the analysis is two-fold. First, although Bentham believes that the study of politics, law and society had a moral dimension, his discussion of this moral basis is very much an introduction to those main areas of enquiry. Second, it is worth noting that Bentham's aim in all this is to create a science of legislation and society. For this there are, he believes, three primary tasks: first, to reduce explanations of human conduct to a single type (this he performs through his use of pleasure as the sole cause). Second, to be objective, not to impose his own likes and dislikes, his own standards of value, on the matter being investigated. This, I think, is why 'pleasure' is insufficiently analysed – let everyone decide for himself what counts as pleasure, then the principle of utility can give objective advice based simply on the pleasurable and painful consequences of action. The third element necessary for Bentham's view of science is that of quantification, to which we shall come in a moment.

Before moving on, there is one further problem arising from the two quotations under review. If the principle of utility recommends that we serve the 'happiness of the party whose interest is in question', and if that party is the community, how can this be reconciled with the view that individuals pursue a happiness in which the self-regarding interests are generally predominant? Will not the happiness of the community and of the individual conflict? Is there not a contradiction between what causes an individual to act and how he ought to act?

There are two solutions to this apparent puzzle. One is that there is a natural harmony of interests between the individual and the community: an individual in pursuing his own interests also pursues the community interest or, as Bentham would say, the sum total of individual interests. The other interpretation is that the interests of the individual must be brought into artificial harmony with the interests of the community through the various sanctions – appealing to the pleasure and pain of an individual – open to the community. Let us look more closely at these two alternatives. At first sight both models seem to have been available for Bentham to follow: from the world of economics came the idea of a natural harmony of interests, and from the world of law the idea that individual and community interest must be artificially harmonised. How are we to read Bentham's basic position on this matter? This is clearly a crucial issue with implications for the role of government in society; on the outcome of this depends our view of government as quiescent or as an active creator of the good society. The surest interpretation seems to be that Bentham sees generally a mixture of natural harmony and natural conflict, and that in the area of economics he generally, though not dogmatically, emphasised the former, while in politics, law and administration he emphatically stressed the latter – in these areas it was the role of law and government to ensure a harmony which would not otherwise exist.[6]

We mentioned earlier that in addition to reducing statements about human behaviour to the pursuit of pleasure, and making the calculation of consequences an objective consideration dependent on pleasure rather than a standard imposed from without, Bentham in creating a science of human society also wished to measure or calculate or quantify the pleasures and pains which figured so largely in his analysis. If pleasure is to be the ultimate reality for all social investigation, and if science demands quantification, then pleasure must be measurable. As might be expected, Bentham offers us a formula for calculating pleasures and pains which he calls the felicific calculus. Bentham maintains that units of pleasure and pain can be measured by referring to their seven dimensions – their intensity, duration, certainty or uncertainty, propinquity or remoteness, fecundity (or the likelihood of their being followed by more of the same), purity (or the likelihood of their being followed by the opposite) and extent (the number of people affected). Although he believed that such a calculation was difficult and usually rather loosely followed, the stricter its application the more exact and useful the moral, legislative or judicial judgement which would follow. In principle, pleasures are comparable, as are pains, and a happy life or a happy community is one which uses rational calculation in comparing the consequences of alternative courses of action.

This then in outline is Bentham's principle of utility, designed as a basis for further investigation into what we would now call the social studies. One point is worth making before we continue: the principle itself is not provable, providing as it does the basis for proving everything else. We cannot prove that all men pursue pleasure except at the risk of tautology; put differently, we cannot maintain that all men always pursue pleasure unless everything they are seen to pursue is defined as pleasure. Bentham is aware that proof is impossible but gives grounds for accepting it as a coherent view of the world by pointing to what he sees as its untenable alternatives. Is not happiness or utility a better standard for mankind than its opposite, or an arbitrary, confused mixture of the two, dependent on personal whim, caprice, tradition or custom?

Before seeing how Bentham applies this principle – that happiness is the end of human life, and that if the community is involved the greatest happiness of the greatest number is the proper standard – there is one point worth stressing. This is that the theory refers to individuals. All questions of a political or social nature are questions about individuals; all other terms, like community, are fictions, reducible to individuals. Thus the interest of the community is the sum of the interests of the individuals composing it, and calculations of community interest are calculations of individual interests. The individual is the reality, and government and law must recognise this. As we shall see, Bentham's analysis of politics and his suggestions for reform are based on this belief in individualism. The purpose of government and law is to bring about the greatest happiness for the greatest number of individuals. How does it do this?

Let us look first at the field of law, Bentham's main interest. In order to make behaviour conformable to utility there are four sanctions which can operate: the physical sanction or the natural pleasure or pain which results from an act; the political sanction or that imposed by the ruling power in a state; the moral sanction or that of popular opinion; and the religious sanction. The law inflicts the political sanction (punishment) for offences to the happiness of the community. Two things must therefore be attended to: the definition and classification of offences, and the definition and allocation of punishment.

This rational approach to law, designed to replace the existing mixture of statute and common law, was an attempt to found a code, a system completely derived from the single principle of utility. Let us see first that area which the law should not enter. Both law and morality have the one end in common, happiness, but there is a part of a man's duty – his duty to himself, what we can call prudence – which can safely be left to the individual. In addition there is the area of duty to others. Here the law does enter, as the social motives cannot be relied on without the extra sanction provided by law. Even here the law is mainly concerned with a man's negative duty – not to harm another – rather than his positive duty – to help others. There seems to be a strong sense of anti-paternalism here, of a desire not simply to codify and clarify the law but also to restrict it. There are two reasons for this: one, that Bentham believed that the individual is the best judge of his own happiness, the other that there are cases in which punishment ought not to be inflicted. Punishment, being painful, is defined within the utilitarian perspective as an evil which to be justified must exclude some greater evil.

If we examine this more carefully we shall see that there are four areas where punishment is not called for[7]:

1. Where it is *groundless*; where there is no mischief for it to prevent; the act not being mischievous upon the whole.

2. Where it must be *inefficacious*; where it cannot act so as to prevent the mischief.

3. Where it is *unprofitable*, or too *expensive*; where the mischief it would produce would be greater than what it prevented.

4. Where it is *needless*; where the mischief may be prevented, or cease of itself, without it: that is, at a cheaper rate.

It is worth examining these cases in more detail as they affect the debate as to how far utilitarianism is liberal in its tendency even if not inherently liberal in its doctrine. First, cases in which punishment is groundless: if an act causes no mischief, as for example where the person whose interest it concerns gave his free and fair consent to it, then no punishment should be imposed, or if mischief or unhappiness were caused but it was outweighed by the production of a greater benefit, or where whatever mischief was caused can be adequately compensated for.

There are also those cases where, though mischief is caused, punishment would be inefficacious. Bentham has in mind here cases where the punishment was not established until after the act was done, or where the punishment was established but was not known, or where it could have no effect on the individual, through infancy, insanity or intoxication; also where the punishment could have no effect on a particular act, as where the individual did not intend the act, or did not see its results, or thought they would be outweighed by a greater good. Lastly in this section, punishment is inefficacious where the will or the body of a man is subject to a dominant influence or compulsion outside himself.

Where punishment does have grounds and where it would be efficacious, it might nevertheless be unprofitable – the punishment would cause more harm than the offence does, either generally or on particular occasions. Lastly, punishment is needless where the mischief can be prevented at a cheaper rate, for example by persuasion or instruction.

So the individual is left free to pursue his own happiness, with the law regulating his actions mainly in the field of his negative duty to other men. Where his actions do cause mischief to others and where punishment is worthwhile, its object is to prevent offences by threatening just sufficient pain to outweigh the pleasure gained from that offence. In this way our actions in pursuit of our own happiness will be rendered conformable to the happiness of others.

What exactly does Bentham have in mind when he talks of the happiness, interest or benefit which man pursues under a system of law? Seen from a community point of view, happiness can be analysed into four elements: subsistence, abundance, equality and security. It is the latter which is the chief concern of law, being a product of it; it is a primary task of the law to establish and protect the individual's right to person and property. Generally speaking, the other areas are best left alone. Each man can be left to provide his own subsistence; similarly for abundance: the motives in men are strong enough without government interference. This view does not rest on any intrinsic belief in economic freedom; Bentham simply thought that such freedom worked, that it would lead to happiness. At first sight this seems to conflict with his belief that the law should seek to reduce inequality. Inequality is regarded as an evil because through it the inferior loses more than the superior gains and thus happiness in total is reduced. However, to proceed to such a reduction in inequality would conflict with security of person and property, which is the primary aim of the law, and thus must be avoided, or at least must take a low priority where it might have an effect on property expectations. In general, in economic matters Bentham takes the view that natural harmony will prevail, though he is also aware of natural conflicts and certain natural disadvantages resulting from the system. His adoption, however, of a legal view makes him reluctant to intervene in ways which might threaten that primary creation of the law – security.

We have now looked at the utilitarian view of happiness and of law as the essential instrument in the protection of each individual's pursuit of that happiness. In turning to government it is clear what the utilitarian view would be: first, that the proper purpose of government is the greatest happiness of the community but, secondly, that the actual state of affairs is one in which the rulers pursue their own interest in conflict with this. Just as in the individual the self-regarding interest is predominant, so too in government. The problem therefore is one of bringing the particular interests of rulers into accordance with the universal interest. Such a community of interest is only possible through representative democracy, where representatives of the whole community superintend and control those who administer public affairs. For Bentham such control is only possible through a system in which the secret ballot, universal suffrage, equality of the suffrage and annual elections all exist. Bentham enters into great detail as to how to make such a system practically efficient – as we shall see in the next section – but let us look closer now at the most well-known utilitarian argument for representative democracy, that presented by James Mill in his *Essay on Government*.

James Mill was born in Scotland in 1773, moved to London in 1802, met Bentham in 1808 and became the leading advocate of radical utilitarianism. While Bentham was the main figure in the school of philosophic radicals, and while he wrote endlessly, he published relatively little in his own lifetime, and it was James Mill who was the leading propagandist of the group. His essay on the need for democracy was an attack not only on the existing state of the constitution upheld by the Tories, but also a radical attack on the Whigs' caution about where reform might lead. The most striking aspect of Mill's essay is the shift of emphasis away from the traditional question of who should rule to the question of how to restrain and control the rulers, whoever they are:

> All the difficult questions of government relate to the means of restraining those in whose hands are lodged the powers necessary for the protection of all from making bad use of it.[8]

Let us consider the argument leading to this key question, and Mill's solution to it. Government is necessary because in order to subsist and seek pleasure men must labour, and a situation of insufficient abundance gives rise to dispute and injury. The aim of government is to ensure to every man the greatest possible produce of his labour. To government is delegated the power to protect all, but that which gives rise to government – the need for protection – equally applies to government itself: we must establish securities against the abuse of power by government just as government establishes restraints on abuses by individuals. No simple form of government can be relied on – direct democracy because of its impracticability, aristocracy and monarchy because they set up a sinister interest in opposition to that of the community. Neither can a mixed form of government be relied on, because given the opposing interests of king, aristocracy and people a genuine balance is an impossibility. The only form of government which can protect the individual and in which there is security for good government is a representative system, where an identity of interest is created between the representative body and the community, and where the representative body is supreme.

To create this identity of interests, representatives must only hold office for a limited period, and they must be chosen not by the few but by the community whose interests they represent. Bentham was clear on this point – that all must have the vote, the pauper and the rich man, women as well as men (though in practice this might not yet be acceptable). Mill, however, believes it possible to exclude certain categories of people: women and children whose interests are included in those of other individuals; those under, say, forty years of age; possibly there may be an argument over property qualification. The result would be a system of government based on the middle rank of society. It would provide the leadership and the dominant influence, however wide the franchise. Such a reformed government would pursue utility as its goal and carry out the various reforms, especially in the area of law, which utility dictated. This is the very purpose of representative institutions. However, what assurance was there that this would indeed be the case? Would the people so recognise their self-interest as to rationalise and codify the law, protect property and respect individual rights and freedom in self-regarding matters? Could not the people act in a misguided way? If the poor were in a majority, and if individuals always pursue self-interest, might they not threaten the security of person and property which it was the business of law to defend? If this were the case the utilitarian argument for representative democracy would collapse. There were four answers given by the utilitarians to this pessimistic critique.

First, they believed that rational men would act on their long-term interests which were compatible with general utility, not on short-term desires. Thus property would be maintained since it was in the long-term interest of rich and poor alike. Second, history provided no evidence that the poor would plunder once they held power. Third there was Mill's point, already noted, that the middle ranks would provide the leadership for the lower ranks in any new system. However, there was some uneasiness in these arguments, as shown by the necessity of a fourth reply, that education would show men what their real, rational, long-term interests were. Through their increase in intelligence, men would begin to act rationally, give the long term priority over the short term and recognise their interdependence with other men. 'Self-interest' as the motive of human action now becomes 'enlightened self-interest'; it is ignorance, not poverty, which threatens the social structure.[9]

If such a system of government were set up there is one further crucial safeguard necessary, that is, liberty of the press. Thus the utilitarian distrust of government continues even where the government is properly chosen; the few always pursue their own advantage at the expense of the many and though regular and frequent elections minimise this risk they do not altogether abolish it. Freedom of the press is the main additional check to the defects and abuses of government; so important is it that free and frequent elections without it would probably not serve their purpose. Without a free press the knowledge of government activity necessary for good choice is absent. In a bad government, a free press serves its purpose by 'creating discontent'; where a good one is possible it uses knowledge to combat sinister interest. The people must be able to know whether the powers it has delegated have been treacherously employed or not, and for this a free press is a necessity. Control is impossible without knowledge, and knowledge is impossible without freedom. The alternative is to impose restraints on the liberty of the press and once government discriminates between those who shall and those who shall not publish their views then that government is despotic. A despotic government encourages ignorance and this in turn secures bad government. Mill sums up his belief in the link between freedom, truth and good government as follows:

> We have then arrived at the following important conclusions – that there is no safety to the people in allowing any body to choose opinions for them; that there are no marks by which it can be decided beforehand, what opinions are true and what are false; that there must, therefore, be equal freedom of declaring all opinions, both true and false; and that, when all opinions, true and false, are equally declared, the assent of the greater number, when their interests are not opposed to them, may always be expected to be given to the true.[10]

Thus although freedom of discussion might be seen as a secondary good, serving utility, nevertheless it is a necessary good, without which utility through good government is impossible.

These then are the general principles and values with which the utilitarians approached the questions of society, government and the individual, and they provided the key to the reform of government in order to create harmony between the individual and society. However, the distinctive feature of Benthamite utilitarianism or philosophic radicalism was the carrying into detail of the principles arrived at in general, and we must turn in the next section to their more precise proposals for reform stemming, as they believed, from these general principles. One feature of the general utilitarian perspective we ought to notice is that it is committed to methodological individualism. There is, however, no necessary implication from this of political or moral individualism, and the question of how far Benthamism allows political and moral collectivism remains at the moment unanswered. All we have seen so far is the importance of liberty, not as an independent principle, as it was to become for later liberals, but as a subordinate element in good government. Utility or happiness remains the key criterion for judging a good society.

PRACTICAL PROPOSALS

As we have seen, one of the most urgent reforms, and one from which others were expected to flow, was the reform of parliament. We have seen the utilitarian argument in favour of representative democracy; what we need to see here is that the utilitarians were not content to rest with this general argument. Bentham saw the necessity for detailed examination of the constitutional arrangements whereby popular control would be brought about, and his *Constitutional Code*[11] is a thorough examination of such institutions. First it was important to have only one chamber, elected by the people or what Bentham calls the 'constitutive authority'. Any other system would act as an obstacle to democratic power; thus a second chamber would be dangerous if it were undemocratic, and superfluous if it were representative. The people should exercise their power through elections of representatives, secretly and annually chosen; further, a majority of electors in any constituency should have the right to recall or prosecute their representative. The legislature once elected would be omnipotent: there were to be no checks on it, such as vetoes, bills of right or judicial review. The legislature, checked only by the people, was in turn to check the executive, made up of the administrative branch and the judiciary.

It is in describing the administrative branch that Bentham is at his most novel and detailed. He is referring here to the Prime Minister, chosen by the legislature, and the ministers chosen by him, who would not be political leaders but servants of the legislature. Bentham's approach to the administration is one of maximising aptitude and minimising expense. By the first of these, he means that those performing the tasks of government should be the most qualified; thus a health minister should know about medicine, a foreign minister speak foreign languages, and so on. A rigid examination system would be set up to select the best candidates. As well as this intellectual test there would also be a moral examination designed to ensure the minister's subordination to the principle of utility expressed by popular power. In addition to choosing the best, Bentham also wants the cheapest system and he obtains this by a competition among the equally qualified candidates to discover who will accept the lowest salary for the post.

Once the government or rather the administrative branch has been chosen, the approach of the legislators and of the people to it should be one of distrust. Minimise confidence and maximise distrust is Bentham's advice as regards government. All ministers and officials must be responsible and accountable and to this end administration must be open to public scrutiny to prevent inefficiency or corruption. In fact the major control over abuse in a democracy is publicity and public opinion; without them punishment for corruption tends to be a dead letter. The more public the system the greater the democractic control and the less the corruption.

Such a system is the goal of reform. As we have seen from James Mill's *Essay on Government* the utilitarians were prepared to accept less than this as a first step. Secrecy of the ballot, universality and equality of the suffrage, and annual parliaments might be the Benthamite ideals, but the utilitarians settled at this stage for an extension of the suffrage to make parliament more representative of the whole people. However, it was clear to most that the logic of their position took them further than James Mill's fairly moderate demands for middle-class participation. Thus even those Whigs who appreciated the need for reform denied the utilitarian case for it, worried as they were about the extension of suffrage to those without property. Macaulay's criticism of the utilitarian case for reform was one of the most powerful and comprehensive and he saw that its tendency was extreme even if its immediate proposals were relatively moderate. Macaulay[12] argued against the radical proposals, more for what he believed was their mistaken logic than for any objection to extending the suffrage to the middle classes. He was in favour of reform in order to represent at the political level new forms of property which had emerged over time in society, but not reform based on the idea that each individual was the best judge of his own interest. Macaulay attacked both the method used by the utilitarians – that of deducing what was needed from a basic view of human beings instead of looking at history to see what had happened and what was likely to – and also their basic view of human nature itself – that men's actions are determined by their interests.

For Macaulay, history is a better guide as to necessary and possible reform and it also indicates the variety of human character and motives in different ages and circumstances. No general case for reform can be made out; only a case geared to time and place. Furthermore, Macaulay challenges the utilitarian optimism that democracy will produce the desired result – utility or general happiness. If men always pursue their own interests why should not the poor plunder the rich? If they do not do so, it will be because the theory – that all men pursue their own interest – is wrong. Macaulay's critique was damaging to the utilitarian case and, as we shall see, it was to be his rather than Benthamite logic which was the more influential; what remains to be seen in the next section is the influence of the radicals in the drive for reform, whether or not it took the desired logical form.

Let us turn now to the reforms which utility would dictate once the government had been reformed: the primary area would be that of legal and penal reform. We have already seen Bentham's approach to the limits of legislative interference in general – the distinction between morality and law and the view of punishment as protection of the community, the imposition of which is justified only to prevent greater harm. Let us look at this view in greater detail. Once offences have been defined and classified – and Bentham is a great innovator in codifying the law to abolish confusion, vagueness and ignorance in this area – then the law has two objects: to repair the evil done, and to prevent its recurrence. In the first case the reparation or satisfaction obtained is intended to compensate for the pain suffered; in the second what is called for is preventive measures or penal remedies. In this latter sphere of punishment the aim is prevention, either through incapacitating the offender, reforming the offender or deterring the potential offender.

Where punishment is inflicted it must be economical: no more pain must be produced than is necessary to outweigh the pleasure gained, in order to prevent further evil. The exact measure of punishment and the kind of punishment imposed will vary according to circumstance, but the variation will be based on a scientific evaluation of the consequences of the offence. How does this reflect on those punishments being used in Bentham's own day? The most extreme form was, of course, capital punishment and there were at this time over 150 offences for which the capital penalty, public execution, might be given, from minor offences against property to murder and treason. Bentham believed that capital punishment was not justified, being efficient in only one of the aims of the penal law, incapacitation, but not in the other three: deterrence, reformation and compensation. Corporal punishment (whipping, the pillory, the stocks) is largely unsuitable, as is branding and mutilation of various kinds (practically obsolete). Transportation fails the tests of legitimate punishment in a way similar to capital punishment. With regard to imprisonment Bentham believed that prisons were almost without exception depraved and depraving; wickedness rather than virtue was taught there; accused persons, criminals, debtors, young and old, men and women and sometimes lunatics were all incarcerated in vile conditions, dirty, foul, diseased and vicious.

Bentham's alternative was his model prison, the Panopticon,[13] where labour would make honest men of rogues. The most obvious feature of this prison was architectural: the building was to be circular with the governor at the centre and the prisoners' cells at the circumference, all capable of constant observation. The prisoners were to be taught to work. The management would take a share of the profits and thus would have an interest as well as a duty in promoting industry and good habits. Thirdly, the management was to be equally responsible for the lives, safety, health and basic education of those under its care. Not only would this punishment be economical, it would satisfy all the aims for which punishment is properly instituted – incapacitation, deterrence, reform and compensation. Nor did Bentham believe that such a Panopticon scheme need be limited to prisons: it could be applied to factories, hospitals, schools and poorhouses. Supervision combined with industry would 'solve' the problems of the poor as it would those of the criminal.

If we look next at the utilitarian views on poverty we can see a similar concern for economic and effective action combined with improvement of the individual. Given that subsistence is one of the ingredients of happiness at which the community should aim, then poverty is an evil, and the State has a duty to intervene when individuals fail to maintain themselves. Public relief is essential and to be efficient it must be seen in national terms. A central independent authority checked by government is necessary to draw up uniform rules and to inspect and control their application. Large-scale local Panopticon poorhouses based on labour would deal with the poor economically while encouraging industry, frugality and self-improvement. In order not to make poverty and the poorhouses positively attractive, conditions for paupers must not be better than those enjoyed or suffered by the independent poor. People should not be encouraged to go on relief by entering the workhouses, and in addition conditions should not be so generous as to deny the system the possibility of making sufficient profit to be self-supporting. Nevertheless, in terms of education, health and security the poor inside were better off than those outside, if they could tolerate the strict detailed supervision and loss of independence. Thus, though the government had a duty to intervene to provide subsistence for those unable to do so themselves, it should in return demand labour from those able to perform it and it should organise relief in institutions isolated from the rest of the community.[14] Such a system should protect the poor, young and old, from the disadvantages of the free market economy, and with the right education equip those who could work to enter or re-enter gainful employment.

We have seen how in order for democracy to work, for prisons and poorhouses to be effective, education is of major importance, but we have not specified in any detail what this comprised or how it should be organised. First, there should be a national system free from religious control. Where there was ignorance and poverty central intervention was necessary to establish an educational system. Any danger of despotic abuse would be guarded against by the increase in literacy and by a free press; without state aid to erect school buildings and to help with salaries universal education was not possible and ignorance and misery would continue. The schools, both primary and secondary, would be run on the monitor system, with the older or more advanced pupils instructing the younger and less advanced. Although this idea was already in use in two systems – that of the Anglican Bell and that of the Nonconformist Lancaster – the utilitarians adapted it for purely intellectual, not religious, purposes and extended it to secondary education. In terms of educational content the utilitarians believed, naturally enough, that the system should be geared to what is useful. Education was after all the discovery of a world in which pleasure and pain are the realities, and the investigation of the best means to secure them; start then with what is likely to be of most service to this enterprise. Once the basic skills have been learnt, attention should be paid not to the scriptures, not to dead languages, but to natural science and modern languages. Within the students' capacity to learn, teach the most useful things first. Thus whenever the education ended it would have been valuable; not only would useful knowledge have been gained but the powers of reasoning and criticising would have been stimulated, thus increasing the power of judgement and the likelihood of making decisions conformable to utility.

In the case of pauper children, education was designed as a means of raising them from their outcast position; in addition to basic intellectual instruction, technical education would equip them to become independent employable citizens. Similarly, prison education would be geared to returning the individual to society as a useful member. Thus the importance of education was not only that it made people more efficient in promoting their own happiness but also that it was likely to lead to that enlightenment necessary to bring about the reign of utility. The major obstacle to reform apart from the sinister interests of those in power was the ignorance of the people.

Although the utilitarians had a radical distrust of government power they urged the importance of ordering social affairs through central administration. Nor were prisons, the Poor Law and education the only areas; under a democratic government and a codified law the central administration was to regulate society by supervising and inspecting the work of locally elected authorities in a whole host of areas, including health, police, roads and factories. The government would exercise its authority through inspection, advice and dismissal. The virtue of inspection as a means of control was that it reconciled central authority with local autonomy, producing sufficient uniformity and efficiency yet allowing for variation according to local circumstances. For this to work local government would have to be reformed along the lines of national government reform, and thus popular control plus efficient management would secure improvement in all areas of public life. The intention was to benefit the individuals who comprised society, but to do this government must regulate in order to free individuals from those obstacles to happiness resulting from tradition, neglect, local influence or sinister interest. Intervention was necessary to strengthen the individual – his education, health, safety, security – in his pursuit of his own happiness.

IMPACT ON LEGISLATION

Our task in this section is to see how influential utilitarians were in bringing about the reforms which did occur in the early part of the nineteenth century. How far did their ideas affect the changes that were made in politics, law and society? It would be naive, of course, to assume that where there were changes consistent with the utilitarian point of view, these can be attributed solely to utilitarianism as a body of ideas: there were other influences favouring reform and these must be assessed too. First let us look briefly at the political and social situation in England at the beginning of the nineteenth century.

At the beginning of the century, the population of England and Wales was around eight million and increasing rapidly. The old dominance of the landed nobility and gentry was being threatened as industrialisation accelerated and large numbers of people moved into the towns. It was an age of transition, with the old world of agriculture, small workshop industry and household service still dominating factory and mine, although with increasing tension, both economic and political, between the two worlds.

In the countryside the process of enclosure – dividing the land into separate fields – continued, favouring the wealthier and resulting, along with high taxation and a slump in agriculture after 1815, in the movement by many small farmers either away from the land or into the ranks of agricultural labourers who were subject to the problems of a growing population, bad harvests and rising prices. Many of these in turn moved away from the countryside so that by 1851 half the population lived in towns. By this time the population had also risen to some eighteen million, and it is clear that this major shift from rural to urban living put immense pressure on the towns, organised as they were for a small-scale settled past. This demographic change was compounded by developments in the organisation and technology of manufacturing industry. Machine production not only increased output but also made possible a new form of organisation – the factory system. Together with urbanisation this must be seen as a social revolution. The vast increase in the demand for semi-skilled labour, including as it did women and children as well as adult males, had far-reaching effects on the social structure.

These three factors present at the beginning of the nineteenth century – the move away from the land, the development of industrialisation and the growth of population – put enormous strain on a society largely organised for small-scale, predominantly rural living. The many thousands of institutions of local government, developed in an earlier age, revealed a great deal of variety, autonomy, corruption and inefficiency. In the counties urban government rested on the parish system with the ratepayers – in some cases only the wealthy, in others the majority – deciding policy, appointing officials and fixing the poor rate. Some large towns were also governed in this way, though most were incorporated boroughs. There were some 250 of these, usually ruled by small self-electing cliques, in control of finance, both charitable bequests and tolls and taxes, and generally using these for self-interest rather than efficient administration. So in the counties and incorporated boroughs not only was the system inefficient and often corrupt, it was inefficient and corrupt at a time when increasing pressures were being put on it. In some towns there had grown up over the previous century commissions to manage specific problems – water supply, sewerage, police, lighting – but again these were largely in the hands of small groups, more or less unaccountable, and their work, even when efficient, was unco-ordinated and uneven.

Thus while the economic and social structure was changing, the system of local government and administration was still largely geared to small community divisions incapable of responding to the change of scale and the complexity of new problems. The Poor Law, originating in Tudor times, was based on the parish and, with increasing agricultural and industrial unemployment and a growing urban population, was unable to cope with the resulting problems. The growth of industrialisation posed threats to health and safety both within factories and in the towns which grew up to house the industrial workers. Bad housing, lack of sanitation, crime, all grew so rapidly that private charity was unable to fill the gap left by a local government system which was not equipped to deal with these new problems. In addition to these difficulties there was the fact that agricultural changes, industrialisation and population growth were creating a new class structure which made old methods of solving social problems inappropriate. The old paternal relationship based on the social superiority of land, which lay behind poor relief and charity, was no longer relevant. Not only did the newer middle classes not share such feudal sympathies, but the urban working class disliked the old forms of patronage and dependence as much as they did the new forms of exploitation. Not only were land, capital and labour at odds with each other, but each of the groups was divided within itself. Within the landed classes there were gulfs between the wealthy landowners and the small farmers, sharing only their superiority to the landless labourer; within the middle classes there were divisions between industrialists, and within the working classes there was a great deal of stratification.

It was against this complex and unstable background that the utilitarians offered their comprehensive perspective of political and social change. However, as we shall see, they had no monopoly in the feelings of disgust at social conditions, in humanitarian sympathy with the suffering, in their desire for efficiency, nor in their call for centralised reform – others shared some or all of these reactions. In examining in greater detail the reforms which took place we shall have to assess their influence both on the drive towards reform and on the shape which reform eventually took. The first issue to deal with is clearly the parliamentary reform movement leading to the Reform Act 1832, which in turn inaugurated a shift in the balance of political power which led to the reforms in local government, the Poor Law, factories, prisons and education, all of which added to the strengthening of the central state and a diminution of local autonomy.

Criticism of the unreformed system of parliamentary representation was not new in the 1830s. In the eighteenth and the early part of the nineteenth century the call for reform had come from various quarters, from those attacking its corruption to those attacking its undemocratic nature, but it was not until the 1820s that the propertied classes began to attack the system as excluding the new classes of manufacturers and industrialists. Although working-class radicals, the utilitarians, the middle classes and aristocratic Whig reformers all pressed the need for reform there were major divisions between them as to whether limited reform was to be a first or a last step. Further, the utilitarians believed in representation of the general interest as an aggregate of individual interests; the others saw it as a mixture of group interests, social and economic. Thus the Whigs and middle-class reformers wanted to see represented those forms of property then excluded, and the working-class radicals wanted labour represented; the utilitarians alone wanted individual interests represented. However, they were united in their condemnation of the existing system, even though the middle- and working-class movements were never fully united in their organisation or objectives.

Parliament by this time saw the House of Commons as the stronger element, through its claim to be representative and through its control of finance, but with the House of Lords as a powerful partner, or obstructer, especially if it acted with the King in opposing measures. Most of the government sat in the Lords, and it controlled many parliamentary constituencies. These were either counties or boroughs, most sending two members to the Commons. There were high income qualifications to be a member; voting in a county was based on a fairly low franchise, but the elections there with no secret ballot were dominated by the influence of the local landed family, contested elections being fairly rare. Boroughs, on the other hand, were much more varied: most were very small in terms of eligible voters, and most were controlled by peers or the government – only in large boroughs were elections genuine contests. In all, in 1800 only 3 adult males in every 100 could vote, while many large towns were unrepresented. The system was dominated by the nobility, gentry, rural interests, and the Church and, naturally enough, the pressure for reform came from industry, commerce, the towns and dissenters.

On the surface the reform which came about in 1832 was very limited, the aristocracy and landed interests retaining their dominance in the Commons. Many small boroughs were disenfranchised, while others lost one of their two members. New boroughs were created, many of them in industrial towns, but the counties also gained seats, strengthening the landed interest. In terms of the franchise, the vote was extended to more of the middle classes, with many of the working classes eventually losing their votes. Before 1832 some 478,000 adult males were enfranchised; after the Reform Act this number rose to 813,000. It was still therefore only 1 in 7 adult males who could vote, or some 1 in 30 of the total population. The reform then was a very moderate affair; although it recognised new interests these were brought into the system in such a way as not to threaten the older interests. However, even though the reform was moderate it met a great deal of opposition and it was in overcoming this opposition that the Benthamites played their part.

The Whig ministry of Lord Grey was formed in 1830 and Russell introduced the first Reform Bill in 1831, an essentially conservative measure designed to allow the middle classes into the system as junior partners. The Tories opposed the Bill vigorously, seeing it as an attack on the traditional constitution, on the influence of Crown and Lords and as a dangerous precedent. In the second reading of the Bill they succeeded in passing a hostile amendment and Grey went to the country, returning with clear support for reform. This time the second Bill was rejected by the Lords and this led to mass demonstrations and serious riots in different parts of the country. In the face of the King's refusal to create new peers to change the balance in the Lords, Grey introduced a third slightly weaker Bill, which this time passed through both Commons and Lords. However, the Tories again passed a hostile amendment and Grey resigned, the King again refusing to create new peers. Violence and protest again broke out. While Wellington was attempting to form a Tory ministry there was a crisis in the country; in addition to popular demonstrations, there was a run on gold. The King was forced to agree to create new peers and in the face of this the Lords passed the Bill, which became the Reform Act of 1832.

The Benthamites saw their role in all this both as agitators and organisers of protest and also as communicators to the government of the state of public opinion. They believed that the threat of revolution would be sufficient to stiffen Whig resolve[15] and their political activity was geared to making this threat appear plausible through demonstrations, news reports and their influence on various political unions organised for further reform. The passage of the Reform Bill was punctuated by violence and unrest but the utilitarian radicals gave this the appearance of a revolutionary situation by exaggeration and rhetoric. Where there was division they stressed unity, where there was weakness they stressed strength. It does seem then that the Benthamites, especially James Mill, played an important role in supporting reform through the fear of a revolutionary alternative. However, it must be noted that their activities served Grey and the reforming Whigs just as well as they served the cause of the middle-class radicals. The Whigs were happy to use the Benthamite propaganda in their conflict with the King and Tories, so the Benthamites should not be seen too readily as manipulators of the naive Whigs. However, even if the Benthamites were to some extent aiding the Whigs rather than threatening them, it is the case that their presentation of unrest as revolutionary menace did help in an important way to break the opposition of the King and House of Lords.

The Reform Act then was a moderate affair but, its passage having involved many individuals, groups and organisations outside parliament, it held the implication for many that further reforms would follow. However short it fell of the Benthamite ideal of representative democracy, it gave to many the impression of inaugurating a new era of reform and in this, despite the continued dominance of aristocratic interest, it did not wholly disappoint. What seemed the first obvious reform likely to follow was that of the municipal corporations. A Royal Commission was appointed in 1833 and the relevant Act followed in 1835. The Commission examined 285 towns thoroughly and accurately but the General Report, written by a radical MP as Chief Commissioner and a Benthamite associate as Secretary, made drastic condemnations of most of the 246 corporations examined. The Bill suggested one uniform system for 183 of the boroughs, later reduced to 178, with elected councils chosen by all ratepayers of three years' standing. Members would sit for three years, one-third retiring every year. Due to a Lord's amendment there was to be a property qualification for councillors, and aldermen were to be elected by the councillors and serve for six years. Boroughs and towns not already incorporated could become so and thus adopt the new system, now more democratic than the parliamentary system, though with property still retaining a powerful influence. However, although this reform did represent some advance in reducing corruption and incompetence, the actual powers given to these new elected councils were limited. The old powers of the improvement commissions could be transferred to them, but only voluntarily, and this happened only very gradually. However, what the reform did establish was the potential for future extension of local government powers based on accountable elected bodies. This, along with equal household suffrage and annual elections, gives the impression of Benthamite influence, and it does seem the case that the speed and partiality of the Report presented by the Chief Commissioner and Secretary did influence the course of reform. However, though the notions of equality of suffrage and accountability were introduced, albeit imperfectly, the other key feature of Benthamite reform – centralised control through inspection – was not. It is in the field of social reform that this played its greatest role, and the most urgent problems here were factory and Poor Law reform.

The unreformed Poor Law system showed an absence of both uniform policy and central control, and as we have seen its basis in the parish by this time rendered it inadequate as a means of dealing with the problems of unemployment and poverty. To begin with the laws of settlement and removal, whereby individuals could only claim from their own parish and could be removed from others on which they might become a burden, were hopelessly out of date and cruel in a period of rural unemployment, industrialisation, growth of towns and the migration resulting from these phenomena. There had been attempts at reform, parliamentary and local, with regard both to indoor and outdoor relief, but no comprehensive system had ever replaced that established in the reign of Elizabeth I. Paupers were regarded as being of three types, though even here the system was ambivalent, to say the least, as to the distinctions themselves and as to how they should be applied. First, there were those unable to find work, the able-bodied poor, who could be set to work; next, those unable to work, the impotent poor, who needed relief; lastly, those who wouldn't work, the idle poor, who must be compelled to work in suitable institutions. This was as far as agreement went; sometimes indoor relief and punishment included all groups, in other places indoor and outdoor relief were given according to need; in yet other places the Speenhamland system was adopted – that of supplementing wages out of the poor rates.

There were many groups hostile to the workings of the Poor Law on humanitarian, individualist or paternalistic grounds, or simply on grounds of cost and efficiency – the poor rate was becoming an expensive burden on those who supported it. In 1832 a Royal Commission was set up to enquire into the Poor Laws and it advocated sweeping reform rather than retention or abolition. The leading figure in the Commission was Edwin Chadwick, a close associate of Bentham, who was appointed first an Assistant Commissioner, then a Commissioner, and who drafted the report with Nassau Senior, a radical economist. Their Report, which led to the Poor Law Amendment Act 1834, drew a sharp distinction between the indigent – who had to be helped – and the poor, who could help themselves. Relief should be given only to the former category; the latter should not be removed from the labour market. In order to distinguish between the two sorts of poverty, poor relief should be available only in a workhouse and conditions there should be 'less eligible' than outside. Thus the able-bodied poor would be deterred from entering and encouraged to protect their own interests by gaining employment; those who did enter would be those for whom the free market had nothing to offer.

Chadwick's Report and its principle of 'less eligibility' seemed to offer a simple, uniform and economic alternative to the complexity and cost of the old system and it formed the basis of the Poor Law Amendment Act of 1834. In addition to the principle which was to govern poor relief, Chadwick also detailed the administrative changes which would be necessary to implement it. Parishes would have to be merged into unions under elected guardians and run by paid professionals, with a central board of commissioners which would have the power to abolish outdoor relief and direct the unions to build workhouses. In addition to this the laws of settlement were to be abolished, hindering as they did the free movement of labour. Thus central authority and local administration could be combined cheaply and efficiently. The Act itself reduced somewhat the powers of the central board, making it less likely that the eventual system would be as uniform as Chadwick had hoped. The board was not to have the power to abolish but merely to regulate outdoor relief and it could not force local unions into effective action to build workhouses. This in itself made the abolition of outdoor relief unlikely and thus weakened the basic distinction in the Report between the indigent and the poor. Further, the laws of settlement were retained, as was the parish as the basis for financing the system, and without strong central control this promised ill for uniformity and efficiency. What made matters worse from the point of view of Chadwick was that he himself was not one of the three commissioners appointed to set up and control the new system, but was made its permanent secretary. At first sight, the Commission seemed to be acting efficiently: within a year or two thousands of parishes were organised into hundreds of unions. However, the underlying belief that the poor could always find work, and thus that relief should only be given in an institution, proved to be the undoing of the system. In many areas outdoor relief was still given in recognition of the harsh realities of unemployment, while in other areas wages declined as more people were forced on to the labour market. So the system was often cruel if administered strictly; in order for it to be made more compassionate certain aspects of it had to be evaded. The system of local uniformity under central control and inspection, as recommended by Chadwick, was never put into full operation but was established as an administrative model more and more to be followed throughout the century.

It seems clear that in so far as the Act followed Chadwick's Report it was a Benthamite piece of legislation, both in the principles to be operated and in the administration to set up and regulate them. While there were many critics of the old Poor Law, the actual structure of reform followed the Benthamite proposals rather than any other. The belief that it was individuals that were being dealt with, not social or economic problems outside the control of individuals; that it was only failed individuals who needed aid and that they should receive it isolated from society; that efficiency and uniformity demanded central control and inspection; all these ideas together were characteristic of the Benthamites but not, taken together, of other reformers, whether political or administrative. Thus while the purpose of reform was individualist – to free the poor and aid the pauper – this demanded an increased use of the State as a central authority, as the Benthamites had emphasised.

This idea of control through inspection also emerged in the reform of legislation referring to factories, and though no system comparable to the Poor Law commissioners was set up, a Benthamite influence appears to be present in this field too, again not in the pressure for reform but in the detailed proposals. Indeed, the main supporters of reform were working-class groups and Tories, united in their opposition to the manufacturing classes. The problem centred around the employment of children, an essential element of most factory productions. Children were employed from as young as six years old for as long as sixteen hours per day, depending on the industry. Agitation centred on the textile industries and was led by working-class organisations and certain humanitarian and paternalistic Tories – Oastler, Sadler and Lord Ashley. The aim was a ten-hour day, and the Ten Hour Movement saw an alliance between working-class radicals and Tories, the latter taking the lead in parliament – after previous attempts earlier in the century a Bill was introduced in 1831 to prohibit employment under the age of nine and set a limit of ten hours a day below the age of eighteen – while the alliance agitated for reform in Yorkshire and Lancashire with meetings, demonstrations and publications. Sadler's Bill of 1831 failed and a new one was introduced in 1833, after the Reform Act, by Lord Ashley. The result was a Royal Commission, engineered by the manufacturers to delay legislation. On this commission were several Benthamites and it was dominated by Chadwick, who in the Report suggested no employment before the age of eight or nine, and a limit of eight hours a day until the age of thirteen; after that they were to be as unregulated as adults. Those children in employment were to receive three or four hours compulsory daily education. The Benthamite touch came in with the proposal for inspectors to be appointed to enforce the scheme. Though inspectors had been envisaged before, these were now to be independent of the local magistrates and as a board were to report directly to the government. The proposals disappointed the Ten Hour Movement, leaving those over thirteen years old unprotected and, by introducing the eight-hour shift for those under thirteen, making a reduction in adult working hours more difficult. The Act, based on Chadwick's Report, was passed in 1833: no employment below nine years old; below thirteen, not more than forty-eight hours a week and nine in any one day; and in addition, below eighteen, not more than sixty-nine hours a week and twelve in any one day. Night work was ruled out for all those under eighteen, and for those below thirteen education was to be compulsory. This applied to all textile factories, excluding lace and, in some cases, silk. To enforce its provisions, four inspectors were appointed to check on the ages, hours and education of the child workers and report to the Home Department. Enforcement was to prove difficult, especially given the unpopularity of the Act, and the early inspectors were by no means industrious, efficient or honest, so that by 1840 the whole question had to be re-examined and in 1844 a new Act was passed. The important point to note is that though from 1833 onwards there were to be changes in the detail of the restrictions imposed, what was accepted was that state intervention was necessary and, importantly from the point of view of the Benthamite contribution, that such state regulation could only be effective through a system of inspection.

Such a principle was also applied in other fields. The Prison Act of 1835, while not adopting Bentham's Panopticon scheme, and while leaving administration in local hands, did set up a central inspectorate to supervise and report to the government. In education, although no national system was set up, apart from education in workhouses and for factory children, grants were given to the voluntary education societies, and in 1839 inspectors were appointed to inspect schools. Similarly, the Railways Act of 1840 gave certain powers of supervision and inspection to the government. Thus while the degree of government intervention was not extreme it was accepted that, where it occurred, it should be accompanied by enforcement through inspection. This was also true of Chadwick's other great contribution to social change – the Public Health Act of 1848. Here a general board was set up responsible to parliament with certain coercive powers, alongside the local board responsible to the localities. Drainage and sanitation were to be community responsibilities but with a central administration supervising their operation.

It would clearly be an exaggeration to attribute all the many reforms which took place in this period to Benthamite influence. To begin with, there are two stages in reform – the pressure for it, and the detail of its implementation. For some reforms the Benthamite influence came in the first stage: agitation and propaganda; for others it came later: in manipulating or dominating commissions.[16] At times this influence was present throughout, but never alone, always in harmony or opposition to other factors at work. But in their consistent approach to government activity, on the need for control by government agencies to parallel any growth in government intervention, the Benthamites had an advantage in terms of clarity and tactics over other reforming and opposition groups. In terms of personalities, while there were working-class radicals and

Tory philanthropists, the most effective were those like Chadwick,[17] dedicated and clear-sighted with a belief in comprehensive reform and bureaucratic efficiency. While his proposals were never wholly implemented, the tendency of many of the reforms was dictated by his influence.

We have seen how reform during this period led to greater government intervention and the growth of central administration, and it does seem, for the moment at least, as though the Benthamite influence was present in the agitation for or in the detail of reform. Yet at the same time Bentham was described earlier as an individualist, as someone who saw the individual as the only reality. Does this conflict with the collectivist measures taken during this period? Not if we see the reforms as an attack on those forces likely to reduce the individual's power to make his own decisions without domination by sinister interest or influence. Thus parliamentary and local government reform is an attack on the dominant interest of land and aristocracy, but the other reforms too include an attack on local vested interests, on traditional habits and customs, and reveal a desire to replace them with rational efficient administration under central popular control. It is the individual's happiness which is aimed at – but an individual freed from traditionally dominating and corrupting social and economic forces. Where the individual is freed from domination and still fails or cannot but fail then society has a responsibility to protect: thus there must be education for the young, workhouses for the poor, prisons for the criminals, all under democracy at central and local level. Thus the eventual harmony produced will be the result of conditions artificially created, and this creation is the work of government or its agencies.

There is a sense then in which this period can be described as individualist, even though the main thrust of legislation is interventionist; it is an attempt to create a society in which the Benthamite model of the individual is actually realised. Nevertheless, despite a general though not inflexible acceptance by the Benthamites of the principles of *laissez-faire* in economic matters, they did promote government intervention in a wide range of social problems. Was it the case though that their influence was as important as we have suggested? It has been argued that on the contrary the changes which came about were the result of the conditions of the time – population growth, industrialisation, urbanisation – and the recognition of these new conditions as intolerable. On this line of argument reform is seen as a response to new needs and demands. It has to be admitted at once that the background to the reforms we have been looking at was of course important; the influence of ideas does depend on circumstances. Nevertheless, new conditions are not in themselves problems until they are perceived as such, and ideas play an important role in changing the attitude of people towards their situation – conditions are not intolerable unless certain values are held which make them so. It is in interpreting the facts as problems that ideas are crucial. In this process the Benthamites were by no means the only influence; humanitarians, philanthropists, radical working-class organisations, Christians, all played a part in shaping the attitudes of the time. The Benthamites were distinctive here only in stressing the wastage and inefficiency of the system as well as its suffering. So although they played a part in the pressure for reform, it would indeed be wrong to credit them with bringing about the reforms almost singlehanded. However, here we need to repeat the distinction made earlier between the pressure for reform and the detail of reform. Clearly the main pressure did come from the perception by many different groups of the suffering and cruelty of the new conditions; it was in the translation of this pressure into legislation that the Benthamites played a key role. After all, pressure can often be ignored, resisted, delayed or channelled elsewhere; indeed, the setting up of Inquiries and Commissions was often an attempt to delay or obstruct reform and was seen as such by those campaigning for reform. The Benthamites used such committees in order to give the demand for reform legislative and administrative effect, and to give this effect a Benthamite dimension. So if we concentrate too much on the campaigns for reform the Benthamite influence will be underestimated, working as it did primarily at this second stage of converting pressure into practice. Thus in factory reform or Poor Law reform the demands were there, and people like Chadwick played their decisive role in determining much if not all of the form which the subsequent changes took: their influence was crucial not at all stages but at the inquiry and legislative stages most of all. Their most characteristic contribution in this area was probably the adoption of the idea of central control through inspection. Inspectors were not new but the idea of centrally directed inspectors responsible to government or a government agency was new to the nineteenth century and its main supporter was Chadwick. Thus in creating the machinery to make reform effective the Benthamite influence is apparent.

Clearly we should exaggerate neither the extent of reform nor the degree of government intervention in this period. Nevertheless the period can be seen as the beginning, however tentative, and for whatever purpose, of the acceptance of government responsibility in a widening area of social life. This acceptance was facilitated by the activity of the Benthamites, who also to some extent accelerated the process by the inspection machinery they devised. This is not to say that the process then continued smoothly throughout the century. In looking at later political thought and practice we can see opposition to this idea of state involvement as well as support.

REFERENCES AND NOTES

1. Bentham, J. (1960) *A Fragment on Government and an Introduction to the Principles of Morals and Legislation*, ed. W. Harrison. Blackwell: Oxford, p. 3
2. Bentham, J. (1960) p. 125
3. Bentham, J. (1960) p. 126
4. Quoted by Mack, M. (1963) *Jeremy Bentham: An Odyssey of Ideas*. Columbia Press: New York, p. 455
5. Bentham, J. (1843) *Constitutional Code* in *The Works of Jeremy Bentham*, vol. IX, ed. John Bowring. William Tait: Edinburgh
6. For a discussion of this debate see especially Lyons, D. (1973) *In the Interest of the Governed*. Oxford University Press
7. Bentham, J. (1960) p. 282
8. Mill, James (1955) *An Essay on Government*, ed. C. V. Shields. Liberal Arts Press: New York
9. Mill, James (1828) 'Essay on Education' reprinted in a collection of seven essays from the *Supplement* to the fifth edition of the *Encyclopaedia Britannica*
10. Mill, James (1828) Liberty of the Press, op. cit. p. 23
11. Bentham, J. (1843) vol IX
12. Macaulay, T. B. (1829) 'Mill on Government' in *Edinburgh Review* XLIX, repr. in Williams, G. L. (ed.) (1976) *J. S. Mill on Politics and Society*. Fontana: London
13. Details can be found in Bentham, J. (1843) *Works*, vol. IV
14. Details can be found in Bentham, J. (1843) *Works*, vol. VIII
15. See Hamburger, J. (1963) *James Mill and the Art of Revolution*. Yale University Press
16. See Finer, S. E. (1972) 'The Transmission of Benthamite Ideas 1820–1850', in Sutherland, G. (ed.) *Studies in the Growth of Nineteenth Century Government*. Routledge and Kegan Paul: London
17. Finer, S. E. (1952) *The Life and Times of Sir Edwin Chadwick*. Methuen: London

Chapter two
LIBERALISM

POLITICAL THEORY

The epithet 'liberal' is one which is frequently used to describe attitudes towards and beliefs about a whole range of human activities from art to religion, sexual morality to economics. The particular concern of this section is to explore the character of liberal political theory in nineteenth-century Britain but we need first to identify the tradition to which such political thought belongs – to identify some of the characteristics by which we can identify such thought as liberal. This is no easy task, since political liberalism covers a wide range of particular beliefs and even in the specific period of the nineteenth century cannot be described as a monolithic political doctrine. Any attempt to construct a hard-and-fast classification, such that only a person who holds to this or that particular belief can accurately be described as a liberal, is not likely to prove useful. Rather we must seek to identify some of the general features of liberal political thought, the particular interpretation and application of which varies between different historical periods and between individual thinkers sharing the same historical period who described themselves, and were recognised by others, as belonging to the liberal tradition.

The roots of modern liberalism are to be found in the struggle for religious freedom which reached its height in the late sixteenth and seventeenth centuries in Western Europe. The close alliance of Church and State in this period meant that any attempt to break free of the fetters of the established church and to establish the right to worship according to the dictates of conscience included an attempt to break free of the existing political order and from the weight of traditional authority. To justify the claim for religious and political liberty it was necessary to appeal to standards which lay outside the existing system of custom and law since this acted as the foundation of the authority against which the struggle was being waged. An appeal had to be made to criteria which were not bound by historical time or particular cultures; to truths which, it could be argued, transcended particular circumstances. Thus there began to emerge one of the general features of liberal thought – the centrality of reason in individual and social life and, through the operation of reason, the identification of human rights. Against the conception of the world as mystical and unintelligible to merely human minds was asserted a view of the world as a rational system operating according to laws discoverable by the exercise of reason and independent of time or place. Such a claim was reinforced by developments in the physical sciences which were demonstrating that nature was not only intelligible but controllable. If this were true of the world of physical objects then it could also be true of the human world, since man is part of nature. This, of course, was a re-assertion of the ancient doctrine of natural law but one which was taken from the narrower confines of theology and applied across the whole range of human activity.

The exercise of reason reveals that in respect of their common humanity all men are subject to the same laws which confer on all the same natural rights. The social order, in which some are in authority while the many are subject, and the system of law by which this is maintained, cannot therefore be pre-ordained and immutable. It is not a natural order but an artificial construct, capable of being judged by an independent standard and of alteration by human agency.

Early liberal theorists sought to explain the origins of civil society in the operation of human reason. Man in the state of nature had sought to protect his natural rights by combination and agreement with his fellows; he had entered into a social contract. The authority of government and the power of the State derived therefore from the decisions made by the individuals comprising the association. Absolutist governments and monarchies claiming divine authority which override the wishes of the people can and must be opposed. Here we come to another of the important features of liberal political thought – the belief in limited government. By this is meant that any system of government must be subject to control to ensure that it continues to fulfil its obligations to the people. Fundamental to this is the concept of the rule of law – society must be governed by laws which have the free consent of the people, which are known, which are applied equally to all members of society including those who govern, and which are alterable only with the consent of the people.

The implication of this appears to be that a belief in democracy is another of the general features of liberalism, but this would be misleading. The most important of the natural rights which civil society should guarantee was, particularly for early English liberal theorists like John Locke, the right to property – indeed, Locke makes defence of the right to property the ultimate test of any system of government. This right to property is central since it is the possession of property which makes possible independent thought and action. Property also forms an important guarantee of socially responsible behaviour – a person with property is unlikely to infringe the property rights of others or to consent to laws which might jeopardise property and independence. Thus we find that when liberals in this period speak of 'the people', what they mean is the owners of property. If liberals feared the consequences of absolute monarchy they also feared the consequences of a system of democracy which would transfer power to those with little to lose, and everything to gain, by absolutist or authoritarian government. What counted as property was of course open to various interpretations, as was the amount of property which qualified an individual to participate in government. As social changes occurred the area of debate widened – nineteenth-century political arguments about the basis on which the franchise might be extended included groups whose participation would have been unthinkable to many seventeenth-century liberals.

Similar changes in the substantive issues to which liberals addressed themselves can be seen across the whole spectrum of liberal thought. Whereas in the early seventeenth-century liberals asserted the rights of the individual against an absolute monarchy, by the early nineteenth century it was the landed classes and a corrupt parliamentary system which were identified as the prime enemy. Later in the nineteenth century it was the machinery of the centralised modern State and the weight of mass opinion against which the rights of the individual and minorities were asserted. As religious freedom was attained and along with it a degree of political freedom, liberal theorists turned their attention to the restrictions on trade and economic activity of eighteenth-century mercantilism. The demand for freedom of thought expanded from a demand for religious freedom into a demand for free individual self-development. The degree of importance which is assigned to each of these areas varies greatly among liberal political thinkers but always it is the individual who is at the centre of the stage and it is by the effects on individuals that moral judgements on any social, political or economic arrangement are to be measured. By the mid-nineteenth century, liberal thought was adapting to the rapid social transformation of the Industrial Revolution and new strands of thought were developing from the interaction between older traditions and rapidly changing circumstances to produce a rich variety of political thinking.

The belief in freedom and diversity which helped characterise liberalism in the nineteenth century revealed itself as much in the differences among liberals as it did in distinguishing them from other political thinkers. As we shall see in looking at some of the major contributors to liberal thought, there often seems as much variety among them as there are shared features separating them from conservatism or socialism. Unlike nineteenth-century utilitarianism, liberalism owed its strength not so much to a unified commitment to a single idea as to the blending of a number of traditions and a whole range of values. If we look first at John Stuart Mill (1806–73) we can see the influence of a number of traditions, we can appreciate his liberalism, and at the same time we are made sharply aware of the ways in which he differed from his fellow liberals. The interest in Mill lies both in the way he gave voice to Victorian liberalism and in the ways in which he departed from it. There is, as we shall see, a danger in viewing anyone, especially Mill, as a typical or representative liberal; indeed, in Mill's case his critique of contemporary society extends to certain liberal assumptions as well as to more traditional and more conservative areas.

John Stuart Mill was born in 1806, the eldest son of James Mill who with his fellow utilitarian, Jeremy Bentham, determined to educate the young Mill in an intensive, controlled and utilitarian environment. From the age of three onwards he was introduced to the various classical, mathematical and modern disciplines. His plan of life appeared to be well mapped; not only did he follow his father into the East India Company but he was also a convinced disciple of.the Benthamite creed, committed to reforming the world. However, his mature work, while retaining something of his Benthamite inheritance, is characterised not so much by the doctrine of utility, by calculation of pleasurable consequences or logically neat deductive arguments, as by a concern for development of character and, most importantly, a belief in the supreme value of individual freedom. The utilitarian tradition is preserved but transformed through contact with other traditions stressing the spiritual progress of man. While a concern for the individual, his education and development, and for truth through free enquiry are a part of Benthamism, they are elevated by Mill above mere utilitarian considerations. Much of the utilitarian optimism regarding the beneficial consequences of political and social reform is replaced by doubt; this stemmed partly from the open-mindedness with which Mill read such works as Macaulay's attack on James Mill's *Essay on Government*[1] and de Tocqueville's *Democracy in America*[2] in which doubts were expressed about the lowering effects of democratic rule. Mill's reaction to such criticisms and enquiries was to accept the need for historical study to supplement the utilitarian emphasis on the principles of human nature. While reason was retained as superior to custom or intuition, it had to respect and allow for historical change and conditions. Thus democracy could no longer be seen simply as a rationally proven solution sweeping away all injustice and corruption; it must be adapted to local conditions and its weaknesses as well as its strengths must be recognised. Optimism was not replaced by pessimism but it became a guarded optimism, an awareness of the high potential in human society along with a recognition of its equally powerful dangers. What would tilt the balance one way or the other for Mill was the presence or absence of freedom and individuality. Given that the purpose of life was happiness – but a happiness comprising nobleness of character, personal affection, social feeling, intellectual development, truth and virtue, rather than simply the subjective preponderance of pleasure over pain – Mill believed that the crucially necessary feature for such happiness was freedom.

In his commitment to the liberty of the individual and in his cautious approach to democracy Mill modified his utilitarianism and gave it a distinctively liberal character. Having abandoned the Benthamite identification of happiness with the mere sum of pleasures it was open to him to concentrate on the quality of life and it is this concern which explains his love of liberty and his awareness of the dangers of popular power. The individual was no longer merely the ultimate reality which made up society; he was now also the ultimate moral reality. Individualism was transformed from being a method of analysis to being a commitment to a scale of values. Society was no longer simply a vehicle for satisfying individual wants but a unit for the protection and progress of individual development.

Mill's mature statement on the relationship between the individual and society appears in his greatest work, *On Liberty* (1859).[3]

This begins with a denial that the coming of democracy would in itself solve the problem of the relationship between ruler and ruled. His father's belief that the key to the prevention of abuse was the principle of constant checks did not do away with the possibility of coercion of individuals or groups. The form of government might affect the details of the problem but not its essential nature, and that problem – the security of individual freedom – would not naturally diminish under a democracy; indeed, when the people became conscious of their power the problem was likely to increase. Democracy might be inevitable, it might be welcomed, but its probable effects on individual freedom must also be guarded against.

Why was Mill so concerned to protect the individual? As we have seen, both Bentham and James Mill believed in the importance of freedom in furthering the reign of utility; what distinguishes John Stuart's views is that he recognises the intrinsic importance of freedom as well as its utilitarian role. Thus while freedom of thought and speech are valued as a means to truth, they are also the essential climate without which truth becomes mere opinion held without rational conviction. Freedom in the realm of ideas is important in revealing error, either complete error or, more commonly, partial error as between two opposing views, but it is also crucial in keeping truth alive and rationally understood, rather than allowing it to descend into dead dogma. For truth to be of value to the development of moral character it must be held freely; the genuine appreciation of truth involves an understanding of error, and for this free enquiry is essential. Censorship is a despotism which not only reduces the possibility of progress but also dwarfs the human mind.

A similar combination of intrinsic and instrumental arguments appears in his defence of liberty of action or the claims of individuality. While there are good social reasons for defending the individual's right to act freely – the more variety in styles of life and action the more possibility of developing improved ones and the greater the contribution of individuals to social progress – nevertheless the most forceful arguments which Mill puts forward in defence of individuality are those which concern the individual himself. Human nature is not meant to be raw material moulded by tradition and custom but a living growth requiring all-round development. Thus for the sake of the integrity and quality of individual life each person must plan his own life and exercise his own judgement by subjecting custom and convention to rational scrutiny. Conformity robs the individual of his human aspects, reducing him to a servile and narrow copying machine. Without individual self-assertion through free choice, not only does the individual suffer but society becomes crippled by mediocrity and stagnation. Although Mill believes in the supreme importance of individuality he also argues for its social benefits in order to ensure toleration from those themselves content with traditional and conventional lives. With the spread of education Mill hopes that those taking advantage of freedom will grow in numbers. Others who do not accept the opportunity must be made to see the benefits to be gained from those pursuing freedom for its own sake. Without freedom progress is inconceivable and happiness and morality are robbed of their essential nature.

Now this is of course to see the problem from the individual's point of view, but Mill is equally clear on stressing the need for social unity. Man is a social animal and this is as much a part of his nature and thinking as is his sense of individual identity. How then to distinguish the legitimate claims of society from the proper sphere of individual action? Mill believed that a clear line could be drawn – society ought not to interfere by legal compulsion or social control unless the actions of an individual harmed the interests of another.[4] Where happiness or morality seemed to suggest intervention this should be limited to persuasion unless the interests of another were involved in a harmful way. This was not a plea for permissiveness or indifference but a liberal plea for toleration – not to abandon moral standards or to suspend disapproval but to express such standards without imposing them coercively on others. Toleration meant allowing freedom to others despite strong disapproval, rather than allowing it because of a lack of such hostility. Now, clearly, if the limits of toleration lie with the harming of others' interests, Mill needs to give a clear outline of this concept. Although in performing such a task he denies himself the use of abstract or natural rights and appeals instead to utility he does take 'utility in the largest sense, grounded on the permanent interests of a man as a progressive being'.[5] The interests to be protected are not simply analysable in terms of pleasure and pain subjectively assessed but in terms of man's nature as a developing member of society. In developing this line of thought Mill does in fact refer to certain interests as 'rights' and in his discussion of justice in another of his works, *Utilitarianism* (1863), he also talks of rights, injury to which justifies interference.[6] Thus although he apparently denies the liberal approach to rights and maintains the utilitarian language of interests, yet in his desire to develop a critical standard by which to judge legal and social interference, his use of a specific category of interests moves him very close to the liberal defence of individual rights. In both cases there is a strong presumption against interference for another's good unless certain injury has taken place: a placing of the burden of justification on those who would invade freedom rather than those exercising it. In this belief that the protection of the individual is a prime consideration of society Mill articulates the liberal suspicion of government, not least the democratic form developing in the nineteenth century.

In its potential danger to individual liberty, democracy is similar in principle to all forms of authority; in practice it might well be even more dangerous. However, there is also a further danger to which democracy is more liable and that is a decline in the quality of leadership due to the representative system. Would not the inclusion of the materialistic, mediocre middle classes or the uneducated working class lead to a reflection of this mediocrity and ignorance at the central level? How could the democratic system be so arranged that the morally wise and intellectually gifted were given positions of authority under the control of the democratic majority? Could both despotism and mediocrity be avoided? More positively, could the need for both leadership and participation be catered for within the one system? Certainly representative government is right to give ultimate power to the people – not least because it is only through the exercise of such power that people are educated into public responsibility – but equally such a government needs legislative and administrative expertise to function well. Mill's attempt to balance these claims sees him limiting the role of the elected assembly to one of control of government through publicity, criticism and ultimately, expulsion, while the government sees to the expert framing of legislation and its professional administration according to the will of parliament. Thus Mill's general approach to reform is to make the assembly as representative as possible – we shall examine some of his practical proposals in the next section – while restricting its role to one of control rather than actual government.

So Mill shared much of the liberal suspicion of rapid progress to democratic rule, though from a desire to protect excellence rather than from aristocratic or middle-class interests. Indeed, it is Mill's departure from the conventional respect for aristocratic and bourgeois forms of property which separates him from many of his fellow liberals and makes him a sympathetic critic of socialism. Although he did believe that the system of private property could with improvement be regarded as beneficial, he was aware how much the idea of property had changed through time, and recognised the need to adapt property to human improvement rather than regarding it as a fixed and absolute right. If the public advantage demanded it then law and custom must be amended to allow changes in the system of property.[7] Thus what many liberals saw as the basis of their creed – the right to property – Mill is prepared to question. In a similar vein he supports the activities of trade unions, recognising the need for working men to combine to combat their isolation and vulnerability when acting as individuals. Even socialism itself, if it could avoid revolution and centralisation, might be a proper context for the material and spiritual advance of a people.

In contrast to Mill, Richard Cobden (1804–65) appears much more typically liberal – typical, that is, of the stereotype so prevalent to twentieth-century critics of nineteenth-century liberalism. He seems uncomplicated, practical and middle-class. Starting with the belief that the individual was the key to social life and his free activities the main element in progress, Cobden applied this to the economic field. The Manchester School, as Cobden and his allies were known, concluded simply enough from this that the functions of government should be limited. Order and security needed to be maintained and free contracts protected but otherwise the life of the community and especially its economic life should be left unrestricted. There might be exceptions, as in the case of child employment, but generally government had only a minor role to play in the material progress of a society. Once the middle classes became conscious of themselves they could replace aristocratic power and remove the fetters on trade and industry. With free economic advance both the middle and the labouring classes would benefit; left to themselves without aristocratic or government intervention these two classes born of the Industrial Revolution would realise their identity of interests with the expansion of trade and industry, and higher wages. As we shall see in the following sections, the main obstacle to this harmonious future lay in the existence of the Corn Laws which kept the price of grain artificially high by restricting imports and so protected the large landowners at the expense of the urban population. It was the campaign to repeal the Corn Laws which brought Cobden and Bright to prominence in the late 1830s and the 1840s. In practical terms these laws were the main enemy representing aristocratic dominance and economic restriction.

Nor was the argument for freedom of trade restricted to domestic affairs. Free international trade would have even greater benefits: to trade itself, to world peace and to government expenditure through a limitation in armaments. The reduction of taxes consequent to this policy of non-intervention would in turn benefit the domestic economy. Colonies should be liberated and commercial ties between nations should replace relationships of military and diplomatic superiority and inferiority. Just as the repeal of the Corn Laws was the key to domestic harmony and progress, so Free Trade was the key to international peace and prosperity. Just as Cobden believed that freedom would see no essential hostility between the middle and working classes but rather the reverse, so with relations between nations in a climate of free competition.

Cobden's liberalism then is a combination of practical thought, largely economic, and a high sense of moral fervour, and it is a similar mixture which appears in the life of W. E. Gladstone (1809–98). Having left the Conservative party over Free Trade in 1846, his economic views were generally those of Cobden and his policies were designed to emancipate the financial and economic life of nineteenth-century Britain. Similarly, in international affairs he was a supporter of Free Trade and suspicious of imperialist ties, though not committed to non-intervention in the Cobdenite manner. Here the moral fervour dominated the practical thinking and Gladstonian liberalism was more concerned with international justice than with mere national interest or non-intervention. As we shall see when we consider the reforms actually instituted by liberals in the nineteenth century, Gladstone was a major figure in the world of action despite or perhaps because of his minor contribution to the world of thought.

The very opposite would be true of Herbert Spencer (1820–1903). In condemning the march of Gladstonian liberalism towards intervention for the public good he held fast to what he saw as true liberalism, the eradication of restraints on individual freedom. His attack on state intervention was placed against the perspective of his own unique view of society. Spencer's early background was radical and Nonconformist and his early interest was in natural science; from the one he drew a belief in individual rights and from the other a belief in evolution. All nature including society is a living organism growing and evolving and individuals must adapt themselves to their social environment. The end of this process will see perfect balance between individuals, each free in his own sphere and responsible for his own welfare; government will be unnecessary. This ideal becomes a standard by which to judge the value of any society. Strictly speaking social institutions and conditions should be judged in terms of their worth given the stage of evolution reached but Spencer was often inclined to evaluate them in terms absolute, not relative, that is in terms of the ideal where government and social institutions would no longer have a role to play. Despite his organic view, the individual rights which will flourish in the final stage of evolution are used as ideals to condemn the present, rather than features which will emerge in the future. There appears a tension, to say the least, between his evolutionary perspective and his adoption of absolute standards.

The goal of society is the equal freedom of each: all government is immoral, all command, whether over other men or over women and children, is vicious; the abolition of government should bring universal happiness. Clearly this was not all possible at once and government was necessary to act as policeman and judge, but its interventions should be kept to a minimum. It ought not to provide poor relief or education, regulate industry or public health, establish a Church or promote colonisation, build lighthouses, run a postal service, nor generally interfere with natural evolution. Society grows and is not made, and adaptation to social conditions must be an individual exercise. However harsh the results and however severe nature's discipline, the process must continue for the sake of the equal freedom of each. If each does exercise such freedom, Spencer believes that the final result will be one of mutual dependence and common welfare as well as freedom. Thus his belief in the individual leads him to condemn any restrictions on him other than to protect others, while his belief in the organic nature of society leads him to assume or hope that such freedom will lead to harmony and mutual respect.

One problem which arises here is how far Spencer applied his hostility to government, which was drawn from his view of the future, to the conditions of his own time. It has already been noted that his absolute beliefs stood in some contrast to his belief in evolution, and he did come to accept that institutions could have a relative justification. Thus some good things – women's suffrage and land nationalisation – might have to wait for the future, while some bad things – government coercion – might have to last until conditions were right for their abolition. This growing conservatism reinforced his severe attacks on the way liberalism had developed in his own day. Instead of opposing state coercion and compulsory co-operation, liberalism had begun to see itself as the vehicle for attaining the public good. Where freedom was once its goal it had now by multitudes of regulations so extended the system of compulsion that it had betrayed its past and its roots. Thus, although Spencer does make allowance for relative social conditions, his own

present seems to allow for almost complete application of his standards. His extreme condemnation of liberalism seems to make very
little allowance for any relative merits it might have. To Spencer,
as we shall see in more detail in the next section, liberalism in using
state power instead of curtailing it had become false to itself.

To Spencer one of those who most clearly exemplified this treason
was Joseph Chamberlain (1836–1914) whose early political career
began in Birmingham where in the 1860s and 1870s he proved to
be one of the most powerful agitators and organisers since the days
of the Anti-Corn Law League. His commitment to free compulsory
elementary education marked him as a dangerous radical and his
electoral organisation of the Birmingham Liberals further marked
him as a powerful one; within liberalism he was to become the leader
of dissent and revolt against Whiggism and conservative liberalism.
Unlike other Liberals who agreed on depicting social conditions in
nineteenth-century Britain as a disgrace, he believed that their
improvement must come through civic and national intervention and
could not to be left to individual and voluntary action. In addition
to campaigning for the redistribution of political power at national
and local levels, Chamberlain was active in promoting a view of the
State as a vehicle for social reform. For him liberalism would be
ruined if it glorified in the commercial prosperity then existing but
closed its eyes to the attendent misery; unless the social question
was made prominent liberalism would not deserve to continue. The
traditional view of removing restraints on individuals had to be
replaced with a view of removing misery and suffering. Thus in
addition to 'Free Church' and 'Free Schools' there must be 'Free
Land' and 'Free Labour'. The alliance thus forged between nonconformity and the working classes would, he believed, be strong
enough to secure power and promote social reform. Democracy once
achieved must reconstruct society in order to deal with the condition
of the masses in both town and country, and in order to achieve this
parliament itself must be reformed to make it an efficient legislative
machine rather than an obstructionist discussion chamber. Once
manhood suffrage and equal electoral districts had been attained
then parliament should carry out the will of the constituencies.
Unless parliamentary reform led directly to social reform it would
be useless. Official liberalism was challenged by this 'unauthorised
programme'; any remnants of *laissez-faire* were to be replaced by
intervention. In order to eliminate poverty, ignorance and disease
excessive inequality in the distribution of wealth would also have to

be attacked. Liberalism had to recognise that the great divide in society was between rich and poor and that its task was to narrow this gulf by political action. As we shall see in the next section, this was no piece of idle rhetoric; the Chamberlain radicals accepted the need for definite practical proposals to put such a dream into effect.

While the varieties of liberalism so far considered were all in their differing ways radical and a challenge to the established pattern, it is important to note also a defensive tendency, represented by a figure like Walter Bagehot (1826–77). Far from seeing freedom as demanding radical action or rational reconstruction, he believed that 'the most essential mental quality for a free people whose liberty is to be progressive, permanent and on a large scale . . . is much stupidity'.[8] Although he was prepared for change he thought it should come slowly, with due regard for the past as well as faith in the future. Thus although he supported the extension of representation to all classes in the community this should be done in a way that preserved the representation of the politically older classes and denied the newer classes the dominance which mere numbers might suggest: reform was acceptable but not universal suffrage, which might threaten the peaceful evolution of parliamentary government. Although Bagehot was a liberal – he stood unsuccessfully as a Liberal candidate in 1866 – he was more in the tradition of Burke, the great eighteenth-century Whig and father of modern conservatism. Like Burke he saw the need for change but change consistent with continuity and not a challenge to it.

Thus liberalism in the nineteenth century – and we have yet to consider the 'New Liberalism' of the end of the century – was a large family. It included perspectives from *laissez-faire* to interventionist; groups who saw their goal as the removal of hindrances to freedom in trade, religion and politics, and those who wised to use the new freedom to reconstruct society to the advantage of the oppressed; individuals who saw it as the embodiment of middle-class values and those who saw it as the hope of labour. Within this wide variety there was nevertheless a firm commitment to the individual, his freedom and his rights; the disputes were generally as to the role of the State in promoting rather than merely protecting such freedom. Indeed it was dependent on whether or not such a dominant role was accorded to the State that such liberals were distrustful or optimistic about the coming of democracy and the entry of the working classes to political power.

PRACTICAL PROPOSALS

Given the sometimes severe disagreements among liberals regarding the proper relationship of the state to the individual, it is no surprise to see similar disputes regarding the particular reforms which liberalism was seen to demand. In the early part of the century when liberals were overshadowed politically by the Whigs they appeared united on the need for parliamentary reform, but even on this subject, as the century progressed and they became the dominant force, there was sharp disagreement about both the desirable extent and the pace of reform. In economic matters too the original unity of opposition to restrictions on trade gave way to conflicts regarding the need or not for state intervention. Similarly in social affairs liberalism failed to develop a unified creed. Its bias was always towards freedom but there were constant disputes about the way to achieve such a goal. Did it imply leaving everyone alone as much as possible? Did it demand help for those unable to help themselves? More radically, did liberty itself imply the need for equality? What were to count as restrictions on individual freedom: acts of government only, public opinion, economic depression, poverty? If economic hardship was a restriction on liberty then clearly there could be a legitimate role for government in combating such conditions; if on the other hand hardship was an individual fault then the government should leave well alone. Liberalism, despite its frequently held stereotype, was never unambiguously *laissez-faire*, even in economic matters.

Nevertheless it is the case that in the early part of the century liberalism saw its role as a liberating one against the restrictions and defences of an age based on the power of land and the status of the aristocracy. With the passing of the Reform Bill of 1832, which gave industry and the middle classes some increase in representation, the main target became the Corn Laws both as protectors of the landed interest and as symbols of protection generally. The Corn Laws had been passed in 1815 to exclude foreign wheat until the price of domestic wheat was sufficiently high; in 1828 a sliding scale was introduced which made some concession to Free Trade but the principle of protection was still retained. With the expansion of industrialisation and the growth and movement of population away from the land the excessive price of wheat caused hardship, especially in the large industrial areas of the north. In 1838 Cobden joined the movement against the Corn Laws and from his entry into parliament in 1841 he concentrated largely on this single issue. The alliance

Liberalism

between him and John Bright created a massive extra-parliamentary agitation for reform. Great meetings were held all over England, challenging the view that parliament could be an independent assembly deliberating in isolation from pressure outside. A parliament dominated by land must be made to see the misery it was causing to the industrial and labouring interests, and the Tory administration of Peel must be forced to deny its protectionist followers in order to satisfy the new forces created by the Industrial Revolution.

The Corn Laws were repealed in 1846, splitting the Conservative party between the Peelites, many of whom, like Gladstone, were to become prominent Liberals, and the Protectionists, who were to carry on the party under the leadership of Lord Derby and Disraeli. If the removal of tariffs did not cause the economic prosperity which followed, it certainly heralded it; both in agriculture and in industry the 1850s were a period of economic growth, and this was the background of mid-Victorian liberalism which dominated British politics until the 1870s. Free Trade seemed unquestionably correct, and even the Cobdenite faith in its consequences for world peace survived the Crimean War and the Indian Mutiny. Progress seemed to be the order of the day and this was linked in liberal minds with economic freedom. However, it should not be concluded from this that liberals held an unquestioning faith in *laissez-faire*.

Usually seen as one of the most individualist of liberal thinkers and one whose prejudice against interference might seem to make him an adherent of *laissez-faire*, J. S. Mill was nevertheless a supporter of government action over a fairly wide area. Where the cost of economic growth fell heavily on certain unprotected sections of the community the government had a duty to aid the sufferers; where individuals could not perform certain tasks themselves the government ought to provide or regulate the services, say railways, gas supply, lighthouses, the Poor Law or colonisation. Again, if individuals could not protect themselves, as with children, lunatics or married women, the State ought to act on their behalf. Again, in some cases like education the public good could not rely on individual judgement but should compel parents to have their children educated, and could even set up a system of state schools so long as they were not the sole providers. Thus, although he maintained a distrust of over-centralisation he saw the need for state action where individual action could not provide certain public services.

We can certainly not conclude from this that Mill himself held a general presumption in favour of state action. However, even the extent to which he did go was sufficient to bring the disapproval of that upholder of older liberalism, Herbert Spencer, who saw every additional example of state interference as strengthening the tacit assumption that the State had a duty to cure all evil and bestow all benefit. Even to make the exceptions which Mill makes to the doctrine of *laissez-faire* is to begin the road to slavery. Once parliament begins to be active there will be no limit to its activities. It is the duty of the liberals to warn against the tendency of the age, even more than attacking individual instances of such a tendency. It is a mistake to believe that some measures can be supported and others opposed; if they involve state interference they must be opposed equally. Liberalism was in danger of compromising itself into nonexistence.

This conflict between the government as the remover of restraints and government as the provider of certain services is a continuing one within the liberalism of the mid-century. If we turn to the politics of the period we can see such pressures at work. The greatest liberal figure was W. E. Gladstone who became Prime Minister in 1868, having served in various administrations headed by Palmerston and then Lord John Russell. The Liberal party which came to prominence under Gladstone was a coalition of the old aristocratic Whigs, the radicals, and the Peelites who had left the Tories over the repeal of the Corn Laws. This uneasy alliance was very much born of parliament; it had little ideological or electoral unity, and thus liberalism even under such a commanding figure as Gladstone was never wholly unambiguous as to its practical implications. While he managed to integrate various social and political movements – especially nonconformity and the working-class vote – into the Liberal party there were always tensions over the proper ends of government action, tensions which eventually led to the breakup of its support.

Gladstone began his political life as an Anglican and a Tory, entering parliament in 1832 when the Tories were led by Sir Robert Peel. His views were orthodox, marked only by strong support for the established Church. When Peel became Prime Minister in 1841 he served under him at the Board of Trade, resigning in 1845 over an increase in the parliamentary grant to the Roman Catholic Maynooth College in Ireland. However, he stayed loyal to Peel both during and after the split in the party over the repeal of the Corn Laws. His views were gradually becoming more liberal over such issues as Free Trade, religious liberty and international and colonial affairs, though he was still a conservative and hoped for a reunion of the party once protectionism became a dead issue. What finally occurred in 1852 was a coalition of the Whigs and Peelites under the leadership of Lord Aberdeen, with Gladstone becoming Chancellor of the Exchequer. His aims were financial and administrative reform at home and peace abroad, the kind of economic liberalism of the Manchester School, but he and the dwindling band of Peelites were still somewhat unsure of their future and he remained outside the succeeding administrations, both the Whig one led by Palmerston and the Tory one formed by the Earl of Derby. It was not until 1859 that the Whigs, Peelites and radicals combined together, even if in the first instance this was to overthrow the Conservatives. In the subsequent ministry Gladstone again became Chancellor, under Palmerston, in a ministry which reflected the new Liberal alliance. His main priorities were financial reform at home and economic but not military expansion abroad, placing him nearer the radical wing than the Whig side of the party. Both these groups were fairly small in number, with the Whigs, wealthy aristocratic landowners, owing their importance to their domination of government, and the radicals to their possession of a coherent plan for reform of established institutions.

Gladstone's support for Free Trade and his hostility to excessive military expenditure were both indications of his commitment to public economy and efficient administration; his liberalism meant financial efficiency, not economic intervention. However, despite disagreements with the radicals, for example in his support for the South during the American Civil War, he was identified more and more as a popular leader on the progressive side of politics. Thus, while he was prepared only for moderate parliamentary reform to even the balance between the working and the upper classes, he was seen as a leader in favour of universal suffrage. In addition his early High Church views were modified and he became more receptive to nonconformist grievances. His public image was now very much 'liberal' despite his conservative social views. The first real test came over parliamentary reform in Russell's administration of 1865–66. The Bill introduced was moderate, designed to enfranchise more of the prosperous working class, and it was only in the face of right-wing Liberal opposition that Gladstone embarked on a vigorous defence of reform, becoming a popular hero with the defeat of the government by a combination of Tories and reactionary Liberals. The Hyde Park riots which followed the fall of the government and the entry of the Tories into government, while they may have put pressure on the Tories to push through reform, impelled Gladstone on the other hand to distance himself from his radical public image.

Liberalism for him never meant democracy, not least because property was seen by him and even by radicals like John Bright as a fundamental qualification for the vote. Even liberals like J. S. Mill who believed positively that the working classes should have representation in parliament were not supporters of unqualified democracy. Liberals generally feared that democracy would lead to mediocrity, anarchy and tyranny. Some, like Mill, advocated plural voting and proportional representation to guard against such dangers and protect minorities; others were suspicious that even a Bill as moderate as Gladstone's had been would open the door to undesirable changes. Could political equality come without bringing about social equality? Most liberals preferred not to risk finding out. As we shall see, the Bill that was finally passed by Disraeli's government enlarged the electorate by nearly one million, more than twice the number proposed by Gladstone, and in the election of 1868 the electorate gave the Liberals a majority of 110. Gladstone now stood as leader of a Liberal party fashioned from many diverse elements: in parliament the Whigs, the Peelites and the radicals; in the country the Celtic fringe, the nonconformists, the industrialists and the working classes. Could liberalism stand for something that would keep this alliance united? Could the party maintain its unity after parliamentary reform in a way that it had failed to during it? Would the Whigs accept not just individual reforms but a programme of reforms? It was Gladstone's aim to keep the party united but would this be possible with Whigs and radicals pulling in such opposite directions?

Gladstone's main concern was the condition of Ireland and he proposed to disestablish the Anglican Church there, to protect tenant rights and to open up university education for Catholics and Protestants alike. At home he was the supporter rather than the initiator of reform in other fields. In education liberalism attempted to combine the voluntary element, provided by religious bodies, with state support where religious provision was inadequate. In doing so it met opposition from militant nonconformists and radical liberals who wanted a universal, compulsory and secular system, and from others concerned to protect voluntarism and the role of the church. Gladstone's own view, though not the one adopted, as we shall see, was that the community should limit itself to providing secular education, leaving religious instruction to voluntary bodies. As it was, liberalism was torn between voluntarism and compulsion, between a recognition of the importance of education and a reluctance to provide it in a compulsory, secular manner.

In other areas the desire to promote equality of opportunity and improve standards, which was one of the motives behind educational reform, also showed itself. The principle of open competition was advanced in the Civil Service, religious equality in the universities of Oxford and Cambridge and the abolition of the purchase of commissions in the army. On top of this liberals urged a further extension of the franchise, the adoption of the secret ballot and the elimination of corruption at elections. While reform at home was aimed at the destruction of privilege and a weakening of the dominance of the aristocracy, to lessen the differences in society but not to destroy them, so in foreign policy liberalism under Gladstone aimed at peace through a recognition of the rights of all nations, and was hostile to domination whether of large powerful countries over smaller ones or of imperial countries over colonies. As Gladstone resisted the idea of an interventionist state at home so he resisted intervention abroad. In both cases the perspective was one of respect for the integrity of the individual unit, and in both cases this allowed for intervention if injustice followed from the actions of others. In Ireland too the need for reform must be heeded; eventually this attempt to bring peace to Ireland led Gladstone to favour Home Rule.

It must be noted, however, that in these three areas – domestic politics, foreign policy and Ireland – Gladstonian liberalism was under constant challenge from the radical wing of the party, especially that group of radicals headed by Joseph Chamberlain who believed in interventionism at home, imperialism abroad and union with Ireland. Whereas Gladstone's aim was to remove unjust obstacles to individual advancement, these radicals aimed at the reconstruction of society; where he believed in a moral foreign policy, they recognised the reality of imperialism; where he favoured self-government for Ireland, they insisted on its equal treatment with the rest of Britain. Chamberlain's 'unauthorised programme' of radical reform included free primary education; full local government for the countries; home rule for all the different nationalities in the UK under the Imperial parliament; financial reform, through graduated taxation and levies on unearned increment, to pay for housing and other social improvements; land reform to create smallholders, if necessary through compulsory purchase; disestablishment of the Church throughout the kingdom; and manhood suffrage and payment of members of parliament. Behind all this lay the belief that the improvement of social conditions could only come about through public action – it was the duty of government to create the conditions whereby people could be happy. Of course this would involve expenditure and in addition to financial reform at home Chamberlain believed the Empire would help provide the funds for social improvement: imperialism abroad would help pay for social justice at home. It is still liberalism in the sense that the aim is to strengthen the individual's power of achievement; it does not question the power and efficiency of free enterprise in economic life; but it does give politics a much more positive role not only in redressing grievances and removing restrictions but in providing benefits and creating improved conditions. The interventionist strategy was alien to Gladstone's Peelite approach but it was a form of liberalism which gained prominence towards the end of the century, despite the loss of Chamberlain and his radical message to the Conservative party over the question of Irish Home Rule.

As we shall see in the next section, liberalism achieved a great deal and, as we shall see in a later chapter, it went on to achieve even more, but the loss of the Chamberlain radicals and the long wait until the party adopted an interventionist approach to social policy meant that it had encouraged by default the separate representation of those classes whom social intervention was intended to benefit. The divisions over Ireland and the Empire may have split the Liberal party, but it was the division over social intervention which in the long run lost it the capacity to endure in British politics. This is not, of course, to say that liberalism did not endure; its varying perspectives, individualist and interventionist, were not to be lost but, unlike conservatism, retained their significance despite the demise of the political party which was originally the main representative of these strands.

IMPACT ON LEGISLATION

As already pointed out, there was no clearly identifiable political party representing liberalism until after 1859 and even then it was a sometimes uncomfortable coalition of Whigs, radicals, moderate liberals, High Church and dissent. In parliament the legislative proposals of the Liberal party were dominated by the leadership of Gladstone from the death of Palmerston in 1865 to the split of the party in 1886. Indeed not only in parliament but also in the country Gladstone and liberalism were inseparable. It was a combination which, far from being identified with *laissez-faire*, could point to a record in legislation which justified its popular image of progressive reform loosening the restrictive shackles of a society dominated by patronage, protection, the landed interest, an archaic legal system and the established Church. Gladstone gave to the legislative achievements of mid-Victorian liberalism a moral purpose and a unity which the disparate elements in the party could never have achieved. It was the disparity within the party which made both possible and necessary the personal domination of Gladstone. In parliament individual liberals appear to have behaved according to interests rather than principle but even in this atmosphere Gladstone was able to give a coherence, expressed in terms of promoting progress, self-fulfilment and individual and social morality, to the legislation which was passed.

He was not always successful in overcoming opposition from within the party nor was he always consistent but it is possible to identify liberal principles in the legislation passed by his governments and the earlier administrations in which he held office.

We begin by looking at parliamentary reform, an area in which the greatest credit is often given to Disraeli for his 1867 Reform Act, with subsequent extensions of the franchise being seen as less dramatic. Two points may be made here: first, that the Liberal Act of 1884 almost doubled the electorate created in 1867 and, secondly, that the Liberal proposals of 1866 played a significant part in the process which culminated in Disraeli's reform. Throughout the 1850s parliamentary reform had ceased to excite popular feeling and though several unsuccessful bills were placed before parliament these involved only minor modifications of the franchise, more often than not aimed at gaining the support of minority groups in parliament during a period of notoriously weak governments. In the early 1860s popular demands for reform began to gain momentum, partly due to the American Civil War where the conflict appeared to be between the democrats of the North and the aristocratic slavers of the South, and partly due to the formation of two new organisations in 1864 – the National Reform Union and the Reform League – both of which looked to the Liberal party to further the cause of reform in parliament.

In the same year, in a debate in the House of Commons, Gladstone openly gave his support to parliamentary reform, stating that 'every man who is not presumably incapacitated by some consideration of personal unfitness or of political danger is morally entitled to come within the pale of the constitution', adding the proviso that such an extension of the vote must not lead to 'sudden or violent, or intoxicating change'.[9] It was a cautious statement but one which released a tide of popular support as did the Bill which Gladstone subsequently put forward in 1866. This was a very moderate measure which proposed to enfranchise about 400,000 men, approximately half of whom were drawn from the urban working class. This reflected Gladstone's view that certain sections of the population had demonstrated by their responsible behaviour in both economic and social terms – thrift, hard work, sobriety, the acquisition of property, economic independence and respect for the law – their fitness to exercise the full rights of citizenship. Property was still the fundamental qualification for the vote and still the test by which the possession of other vital virtues was to be judged. The measure would further serve to weaken the hold of the aristocracy and at the same time strengthen political institutions by increasing the numbers of those freely consenting to their operation. The 1866 Bill excited considerable opposition within the Liberal party itself, particularly from the landed interest and from those like Robert Lowe, leader of the 'Adullamites',who feared that it would sweep away all the virtues of the political system created after the Reform Act 1832. Lowe felt that the extension of the franchise in 1832 to a very limited number of the middle class had created a balance between the landed and manufacturing interests which had ensured sound and responsible government by the few on behalf of the many. Gladstone's Bill appeared to open up the possibility of the uneducated and irresponsible using political power to pursue private advantage; those in political power would have to resort to electioneering, canvassing and bargaining for votes, which would only further this decline. A combination between the Tories and the Adullamite faction of the Liberal party defeated the measure, but it was a defeat which greatly enhanced Gladstone's popularity. He became identified as the opponent of privilege, and a link was forged between Gladstonian liberalism and the largely nonconformist urban working class which was to return the party to government with substantial majorities in 1868–74 and again in 1880–85. Gladstone's proposals for reform, though rejected by parliament, contributed a great deal to the importance which electoral reform assumed from 1866, and the desire to undermine the popular reformist image of Gladstone was at least one of the motives behind Disraeli's far more radical Reform Act of 1867 which increased the electorate by approximately 1,120,000 voters. After such an extension of the franchise, the Liberals' 1884 Reform Act, which almost doubled the electorate from 2.5 million to close on 5 million, and the 1885 Redistribution of Seats Act, which created constituencies of a more equal size, were perhaps inevitable. The modern two-party system and organised campaigning for election had begun to emerge, and it was important to both parties to maintain their popular support. There was also considerable pressure from the radical wing of the Liberal party to introduce further parliamentary reform before having to face the next election. Certainly the 1884 Act presents a greater problem than the 1866 Bill in terms of finding a clear application of the principle of limited democracy. While it is true that property was still the basis for enfranchisement, the definition of property had been widened to include male householders and lodgers who had occupied their dwellings for one year before registering as electors. We might conclude that the Liberal view of democracy operated here mainly in a negative sense since many members of the party supported the measure as a means of preventing full manhood suffrage and hoped that the 1884 Act would prove to be a final solution to the franchise problem.[10]

A corollary of franchise reform for mid-Victorian liberalism was the reform of public life, specifically the removal of patronage and corruption from public administration. This sprang from the traditional liberal attack on aristocratic privilege and from the desire to see public life conducted according to clearly expressed principles. The freedom of the individual can only be promoted where the rule of law operates to the exclusion of arbitrary power and where sovereignty lies with the people. Reform was made more urgent by the gradual growth of government activity and the increased spending of public money which necessitated the extension of parliamentary scrutiny of finance and an efficient Civil Servce. In 1853 Gladstone, as Chancellor of the Exchequer, instructed Sir Stafford Northcote and Sir Charles Trevelyan to examine the question of Civil Service reform. Their recommendations were published in 1854 and included the division of the Civil Service into two classes, a higher class concerned with key decisions which required high intellectual skills, and a lower class concerned with the routine or mechanical tasks of clerical work. Recruitment to both classes should be by open competitive examinations conducted by an independent board; promotion should be based on merit and not on seniority. The government in which Gladstone held office fell, and not until 1870 when Gladstone was Prime Minister was the report fully implemented (the Foreign Office remained an exception). Although such reform was extremely important it should not be interpreted as an egalitarian opening up of the Civil Service; rather it sought to create a meritocracy which, given the education system and the social and economic condition of the mass of the population, would remain firmly in the hands of the class most fitted to perform the task.

Significant advances were also made in parliamentary control over finance when, in 1861, Gladstone set up the Public Accounts Committee of the House of Commons and, in 1866, created the office of Comptroller and Auditor-General to scrutinise the conduct of public finance by the executive. The army, where the practice of selling public offices in the form of commissions still remained, was also subject to this reformist creed and in 1871, against violent opposition, Gladstone's government abolished the purchase of commissions and substituted promotion by selection. A year later attention was turned towards the conduct of elections, an area of public life which gave the opportunity for behaviour which at other times would have been intolerable. Bribery, corruption and intimidation were constant features of elections and the public ballot system was felt by many Liberals to make a major contribution to such behaviour. Though Gladstone was lukewarm on this issue it was strongly argued that the political freedom of individuals could only be maintained if the ballot was secret. The proposal was not new – James Mill had argued strongly for it in 1830 – but it excited strong feelings in those in favour and those against. The open vote was defended on the grounds that to exercise the vote was to act in the public interest, while the secret ballot would transform the vote into the exercise of private interest, conferring power without responsibility. Gladstone's position was that his main concern was to preserve the free vote and though he had always supported open voting he was open to persuasion. In 1870 he came out in support of the secret ballot on the grounds that the changed nature of the electorate, including working men subject to pressures from many quarters, made the secret vote the only practical way of ensuring free choice and in 1872 the Act was finally passed. Further legislation to 'clean up' elections was, however, to prove necessary and in 1883 the Liberal government passed the Corrupt and Illegal Practices Act which imposed heavy fines or imprisonment for bribery and limited the amount of election expenses.

If Liberals were active in legislation to reform the conduct of public life, they were considerably less active in the sphere of social reform. For mid-Victorian liberalism the role of the State in improving social conditions was strictly limited. They were not unaware of the poverty and degradation of the working class but the conviction remained that social evils could not be remedied by legislation. Improvement could only come about by the effort of individuals to raise their condition; the role of government was to create the conditions in which the progress of industry and commerce would develop. This meant the removal of restrictions on trade and industry to allow the market economy to operate freely, and there was a firm belief that the benefits of such an operation would flow to all classes in society. Only with the New Liberalism of the 1880s does the concept of restrictions on individual freedom come to include poverty, ignorance and insecurity of income, which it is the duty of government to remove. In the middle period of the nineteenth century 'retrenchment' was the watchword of Liberal domestic policy. By this was meant the desire to provide an efficient, orderly administration following the utmost economy in the spending of public funds. Government had to seek to remove the shackles on economic life but its own services were to be limited and provided at lowest cost. Income tax was tolerated as a necessary evil, preferable to allowing the budget to go into deficit and thereby forcing the government to borrow. If tax had to be levied then it must be done justly and for the Liberals this meant that the poor should bear a fair share of taxation along with the rich, with no group occupying a specially privileged position. It was typical that an acceptable form of government assistance to the working class should be the creation, in 1863, of the Post Office savings bank which offered security to those willing and able to save money. The greatest exception to this attitude towards social reform was the Liberal government's 1870 Education Act which, in the context of the time, represented a considerable increase in state responsibility for elementary education.

The question of education was one which excited debate throughout the nineteenth century, since the necessity of education for the development of individual virtue and social cohesion had to be weighed against the raising of aspirations to a point where they could not be met by the existing social and economic structures. The educated man might read the Bible and come to a fuller understanding of Christian morality but he might also read seditious literature. Education raised both hopes and fears but it also cut across one of the deepest of nineteenth-century divisions – the religious differences of the Anglicans and the nonconformists. The provision of education became the major battleground in which each fought to establish its dominance over the content and provision of education, particularly the education of the working class. Up to 1870, however, the provision of education remained firmly in the hands of voluntary bodies with state involvement limited to the giving of grants to the major organisations providing education. The first grant of £20,000 had been made in 1833, a sum which by 1860 had grown to £724,000. Such a growth in expenditure had necessitated the development of means by which central government might supervise its use. The Committee of Privy Council and the Schools' Inspectorate, both created in 1839, developed into the Department of Education (1856) and became a powerful force in the development of education while preserving the principle of voluntary effort. Indeed, the inspectorate was the mechanism through which the Liberal government sought in 1862 to ensure value for money by instituting a system known as the Revised Code or 'payment by results' whereby schools would only receive the full grant if the pupils passed examinations in reading, writing and arithmetic. In the sphere of university education the main task for the Liberals was to remove the restrictions on dissenters which operated at Oxford and Cambridge. An Act of 1854 allowed dissenters to matriculate and graduate and in 1871 religious tests for teaching posts at the two universities were finally abolished. The promotion of voluntary effort and individual responsibility and the removal of religious restrictions were the major principles of state involvement in education until 1870.

The reasons for the passing of the 1870 Education Act are far from clear. Increasing evidence of the failure of voluntary schools to provide a basic education, the passing of the 1867 Reform Act, increased economic competition from countries with a more organised education system, and the emergence of a powerful pressure group, the National Education League, may all have played a part in bringing the question of state responsibility for education to the fore. Certainly, once the intention to legislate was clear, the government came under intense cross-pressures inside and outside the Liberal party. The education question clearly revealed the variety of interests and attitudes which the Liberal party contained – those for or against compulsory education; those supporting the existing provisions by voluntary bodies or those in favour of state or municipal provision; Anglicans anxious to preserve the integrity of their religious instruction or nonconformists equally anxious to preserve theirs. The resulting legislation was necessarily a compromise between competing interests but the form which that compromise took nevertheless shows the influence of liberal principles.

The 1870 Education Act was largely the work of W. E. Forster and supplemented rather than replaced existing provision. Voluntary schools were to be allowed to continue provided that they could demonstrate that they were able to meet certain standards – they were given one year in which to make good any deficiencies. Where voluntary provision was inadequate the government was empowered to form an elected school board in newly created school districts. Each school board would have the power to levy a rate and, if it so decided, to provide free education and to make education compulsory for 5–12 year olds. Grants to voluntary denominational schools would continue and school boards could assist these schools and pay the fees of poor parents if they so desired. The vexed question of religious instruction in the board schools was eventually met by a clause known as the Cowper Temple clause which stated that in these schools religious instruction would be non-denominational. The Act did not, of course, please everyone and the nonconformists particularly felt that the aiding of poor children at Anglican schools out of money raised by the rates gave a distinct advantage to those schools and forced nonconformist ratepayers to subsidise Anglican education. Similarly the supporters of the National Education League felt that it did not go far enough in meeting their demand for universal, secular, free education. The great achievement of the Act was to lay the foundation for a national system of education and to recognise in principle that every child had a right to a basic education. Compulsion was rejected as an unwarranted interference with individual liberty and responsibility. Similarly, fees were kept on the grounds that their removal would undermine the responsibility of parents to provide for their children while it was recognised that help would be given to those who were not in a position to discharge that responsibility. Central control over education, to ensure minimum standards, was balanced by the continuation of voluntary schools and the local autonomy of school boards. The aim was to bring elementary education within the reach of every child but to do so in a manner which would respect the 'rights of parents; rights of minorities; rights of conscience'.[11]

The most consistent application of principle in mid-Victorian Liberalism is to be found in the area of Free Trade. The removal of restrictions on economic development through market forces could only operate in the domestic situation if similar freedom was extended to international trade. Thus the gradual removal of tariffs which protected special interests was a major objective for the Liberals. The process had begun dramatically with the repeal of the Corn L̶a̶w̶s̶ ̶i̶n̶ ̶1̶8̶4̶6̶ and the Navigation Laws in 1849, to be followed by th̶e̶ ̶ ̶ ̶ ̶ ̶ ̶preferential tariffs on sugar in 1854 and timber in 18̶ ̶ ̶ ̶ ̶ ̶ ̶ was for many Liberals the most crucial area of reform and one which was pursued with great vigour by Gladstone as Chancellor of the Exchequer, particularly in his budget of 1860. In this year Gladstone signed a commercial treaty with France (negotiated by Cobden) by which France removed prohibitions on the import of British goods and reduced tariffs, while Britain reduced the duty on French wines and brandy and abolished those on manufactured goods. In the budget which followed, Gladstone removed the tariffs on nearly 400 articles and in 1861 achieved the abolition of the duty on paper. The removal of the paper duty had aroused much opposition, largely based on fears of the consequences of a cheap popular press, and Gladstone's achievement made a substantial contribution to his popular standing as 'the people's William'.

Free Trade owed its central place in Liberal theory and practice not only to its immediate domestic consequences but also to the contribution which it was felt it would make to international harmony and peace. The Liberal principle of self-determination applied not only to individuals but also to nations; in foreign policy this meant non-intervention in the affairs of other countries and a favouring of self-government for the colonies. Peace in international affairs was demanded by the principle of self-determination and by the domestic policy of retrenchment. War meant increased expenditure and the raising of taxes, interfering with the operation of the market; the need for increased taxation raised the spectre of tariffs and posed a threat to Free Trade. An aggressive foreign policy therefore hit at the very roots of liberalism. The Liberal leadership did not always satisfy the radical demand for a strict adherence to such principles in foreign policy. Gladstone's support for the Crimean War in its initial stages, and later (1881–82), what was seen as his continuation of Disraeli's empire-building in South Africa, the Sudan and Egypt, might be cited as examples. Yet it was Gladstone's reiteration of the Liberal stance in 1876 which brought him back into political prominence. In that year his condemnation of Disraeli's policy towards Turkish misrule in the Balkans and the massacre of 12,000 Christians in Bulgaria gave full rein to the expression of moral outrage and the appeal to principle which formed the basis of his popularity, particularly among nor

If Gladstone's practice in foreign policy did the eyes of the radicals, always accurately reflect a ation of principle, there was one area where his attem blem followed a path from which it was impossible This was the question of Ireland which occupied – temporaries would say, obsessed – Gladstone for over twenty years and was a major factor in the split with Chamberlain in 1886. For all its proximity to the English mainland, Ireland in many respects remained a foreign territory. Intensely Catholic, it was ruled and owned by Protestants but maintained a culture and tradition independent of that of its landlords. The last vestiges of separate government were swept away by the 1801 Act of Union which abolished Ireland's own parliament – a Protestant body dealing with Irish domestic affairs – and made the two countries administratively one body with 100 seats in Westminster reserved for Irish representatives. All attempts to anglicize the Irish met with failure and resentment which frequently broke through the surface in acts of violence. Just as frequently these events were met by demands in England for a stern and coercive response to the disorder. The Irish famine of the 1840s and the failure of Westminster to mitigate the disastrous effects of the blighted potato crops made a further contribution to the intractability of the problems which Ireland presented to successive governments.

Violence flared again in 1865 with the activities of the Irish Republican Brotherhood or the Fenians and once more brought Ireland to the centre of the political stage; particularly to the centre of Gladstone's political preoccupations. Gladstone's attitude towards the Irish question was dominated by his desire to bring peace through a just settlement. Initially he believed that justice for the Irish could only be achieved by allowing a greater degree of self-determination but within the framework of government by parliament. The mechanism by which this was to be achieved was reform in three areas – the Church, the land and education – in which Gladstone put bills before parliament between 1869 and 1873. The first of these, the Church Bill of 1869, which proposed the disestablishment of the Church of Ireland, one of the major symbols of English domination over the Catholic majority, became law in the same year. The Irish Land Bill of 1870, which sought to protect the rights of tenants by restricting the raising of rents and providing for compensation in the case of eviction, also became law. It proved disappointing in practice and failed to solve the acute problems of the Irish peasantry as security of tenure was not effectively increased. The last bill in this tripartite approach to the Irish question was the Irish University Bill of 1873 which aimed to create a new University of Dublin open to Catholics and Protestants, but opposition from both Roman Catholic bishops and radicals led to its defeat. Gladstone's intense disappointment at this did not weaken his determination and when he returned to office in 1880 he resumed his attempts to 'solve' the problem of Ireland.

Violence had again flared in Ireland and Irish nationalism now had a voice in Parliament, organised and led by Parnell. Gladstone's policy was based on extensive reform of the land and local government but there was considerably less enthusiasm in the Liberal party as a whole. The Whig faction believed that the right of landlords had been eroded far enough and coercion was the only sensible course of action, whereas the radicals like Joseph Chamberlain believed that concentration on Ireland was distracting the government from much needed domestic reform and undermining Liberal electoral support. The Irish Land Act of 1881 established fair rent, free sale and fixity of tenure but failed to quell the agitation. Parnell, who appeared intent on wrecking its provision, was imprisoned in October 1881 under the Coercion Act. In 1882 Lord Frederick Cavendish, the newly appointed Chief Secretary for Ireland, and W. H. Burke, his Permanent Under-Secretary, were assassinated in Dublin's Phoenix Park. Such events pushed Gladstone towards a coercive policy in Ireland but he did not abandon his belief that a permanent solution to the problems of that country could be found. Having failed to find that solution in a system of reforms administered from Westminster, Gladstone turned his attention towards a separate Irish parliament and Home Rule – that is, towards the policy of national self-determination and responsible self-government which characterised so many of his earlier positions on foreign policy.

In 1886, in his third administration, Gladstone put forward two bills, one proposing a separate legislature for Ireland which would deal with all matters except international trade, defence and foreign affairs, the other proposing a scheme whereby tenants would be able to purchase land from the landlords. These two proposals released a flood of opposition inside and outside the Liberal party. The landed interest saw the proposals as an attack on the rights of property, the radicals saw them as diverting funds from vital domestic policies in mainland Britain, whilst the imperialists saw Home Rule as a first step towards the undermining of imperial power. The crucial opposition came from within the Liberal party itself where the radical Chamberlainites and the Whigs combined to defeat the Home Rule Bill and bring down the government. More significantly for the long-term alignment of British political parties the Liberal Unionists – those in favour of continuing the Union with Ireland, established in 1801 – left the Liberal party for the Conservative party and though Gladstone returned as Prime Minister in 1892–94 the period up to 1906 is one of Tory domination of English political life.

A thorough analysis of the decline of Gladstonian Liberalism is beyond the scope of this book but it would be misleading to suggest that Home Rule was the fundamental issue which split the party. It appears, rather, that Home Rule provided the opportunity for the expression of tensions which had been present in the party for many years. Gladstone's view of Liberalism and his political skill had been the cement holding the Liberal alliance together, but the reforming creed of the 1860s had, by the 1880s, become a strait-jacket restricting the development necessary to contain the diverse elements within the party. The next period of Liberal dominance, from 1906–1914, saw the reassertion of Liberal reformism but of a more radical and interventionist kind. The traditional Gladstonian view of freedom as the removal of restrictions was supplemented by an attack on squalor, disease, poverty and ignorance as impediments to liberty. In doing this Liberalism showed its ability to adapt its perspective to changing social, economic and political conditions.

REFERENCES AND NOTES

1. For this debate see Lively, J. and Rees, J. (1978) *Utilitarian Logic and Politics*. Clarendon Press: Oxford
2. Mill reviewed this twice; see *Essays on Politics and Society* in *Collected Works*, vols XVIII–XIX, ed. J. M. Robson (1977). Routledge and Kegan Paul: London; University of Toronto Press: Toronto
3. Mill, J. S. (1910) *On Liberty in Utilitarianism, On Liberty, Representative Government*. Dent: London; Dutton: New York. The latest edition is the 1972 Everyman, edited by H. B. Acton (1960)
4. Rees, J. C. (1960) 'A Re-reading of Mill on Liberty' in *Political Studies* VIII. Clarendon Press: Oxford. Reprinted in Radcliff, P. (1966) *Limits of Liberty*. Wadsworth Publishing Company Inc: Belmont, California. For a recent discussion of Mill's essay, see Ten, C. L. (1980) *Mill on Liberty*. Oxford University Press: Oxford and New York
5. Mill, J. S. (1910) *On Liberty*, p. 74
6. Mill, J. S. (1910) *Utilitarianism*, chapter V; see also Williams, G. L. (1976) 'Mill's Principle of Liberty' in *Political Studies* XXIV. Clarendon Press: Oxford
7. Mill, J. S. (1967) *Essays on Economics and Society* in *Collected*

Works, vol. V, ed. J. M. Robson. Routledge and Kegan Paul: London; University of Toronto Press: Toronto, p. 753

8. Quoted in Murray, R. H. (1929) *English Social and Political Thinkers*, vol II. Heffer: Cambridge, p. 234
9. Quoted in Morley, J. (1911) *Life of Gladstone*, vol III. Macmillan: London, p. 97
10. See Wright, D. G. (1970) *Democracy and Reform* 1815–1885. Longman: London
11. Speech by W. E. Forster, 17 Feb 1870, quoted in Maclure, J. S. (ed.) (1973) *Educational Documents*. Methuen: London; Harper Row Inc: USA, p. 104

Chapter three
CONSERVATISM

POLITICAL THEORY

Like liberalism, conservatism in the nineteenth century contains a mixture of different views and attitudes to politics, sometimes revealing sharp disagreements as to priorities, but held together by shared views as to the nature of society. Conservatives have been generally reluctant to articulate their basic philosophy in a systematic manner, due partly to their belief that historical circumstance must affect their response in politics. Thus, although there is a distinct Conservative tradition it is one which usually emerges from responses to more limited problems rather than, as with utilitarianism, being consciously and deliberately premeditated. Such conservative principles as belief in tradition, hierarchy, inequality and authority, tend to reveal themselves in the writings of their main nineteenth-century exponents rather than being themselves the subject of analysis. Within these shared values, however, there are two types of response that can be seen in nineteenth-century conservatism – that which sees change as a threat to be resisted with all the strength at its disposal, and that which sees change as something which must be made compatible with the existing order. Whilst it was the second approach which tended to dominate the work of the main thinkers of conservatism and the leaders of the political party, the first approach was influential in the party generally and from time to time in the leadership. The notion of tradition, so important to conservatives, was used both to resist change and to support it.

Before we examine in more detail the political thought of nineteenth-century conservatism, we must turn to the most influential figure in that tradition, a man of the eighteenth century, Edmund Burke (1729–97) who, like most leading contributors to conservative thought, was in many ways untypical of conservatives generally. First, he was a Whig not a Tory (the term 'conservative' came into use in the 1830s), he was opposed to the power of the Crown, to Britain's handling of the American revolution, and to her conduct of Indian affairs. So at the time Burke supported many changes which the Tory party vigorously opposed. However, underlying Burke's arguments for change was the same rationale as underlay his later arguments against the kind of change that was seen in the French Revolution. All change must be based on the natural strength of a kingdom and the historical and social roots of a people, and thus must operate within limits. It should be based not on abstract rights but on expediency, convenience and custom. Thus American independence was justified but the French Revolution was not; in the former case the Americans were asking for those liberties already established in English principles and traditions, whereas the French were not attempting to reform in a manner consistent with tradition but were trying to overthrow their past. Instead of order built on precedence they were establishing disorder based on abstract rights. Theory dominated over practice, ideals over history, and Burke sees the political revolution as one doomed to failure because of its reliance on principle regardless of circumstance. Whereas the English Revolution of 1688 had been essentially preservative and consistent with the past in its desire to protect the constitution and liberties of the English people, the French were little concerned with the past and thus were likely to embrace extremism in their desire to destroy. Practically speaking, failure was the likely outcome because their simple rational outlook on the world, just as their insistence on treating men as individuals, ignored the diversity and social groupings which made up society. In addition to this political ineptitude resulting from the imposition of rationalism on politics, revolution of this violent and drastic kind was morally wrong. It revealed a wilfulness and pride in refusing to accept limitations on human conduct, a laziness in not attempting any understanding other than theoretical, and in attempting to reshape human nature it challenged both God and nature. Such moral absolutism and unlimited aims would necessitate a savage despotism. Once traditional order and opinion is broken down a new means of social unity must be found which means that government must become stronger and stronger. Without custom discipline can only come by force; the only alternative to tradition is coercion.

Burke's view is that society is not a rational construct like a machine which can be changed or reconstructed at will; rather it is an organic whole made up of partial associations based ultimately on the family. Society develops its own traditions and customs and government must be adapted to society, as man must adapt to God and nature. Man is thus made by society, not the maker of it. His affections, interests, values and obligations derive from his membership of the community. Such an order will be diverse and hierarchical, and the political structure should reflect this. With the long-standing prejudices of a people acting as a social cement, coercion will be needed rarely; consent will be given by the society as long as the government is adapted to it. Thus there need be no talk of participation, natural rights or revolution. The social organism, directed by its wiser elements, the traditional ruling class, can grow and change without sharp breaks with the past. Continuity may demand reform but never drastic revolution; even reform must be treated cautiously. Traditional institutions are likely to embody a great deal of wisdom; their very survival indicated this. Thus no rational test of utility should be applied to customs and institutions historically sanctified. Nothing should be attempted without a clear historical understanding, and such an understanding would point to the importance of tradition, prejudice and society rather than reason and the individual.

Given that Burke did not rule out all change and that the appeal to tradition does not always indicate unambiguously the proper course of action in any given situation, Burke was accorded a position of authority by many diverse elements in British politics in the nineteenth century, both within the ranks of conservatives and outside. A view of society which stressed its organic nature and a view of politics which stressed history and tradition, with the aristocracy providing the leadership, could and did provide justification for more than one type of response to immediate problems; both that response which saw change as a threat to be resisted and that which saw the importance of incorporating change within the general continuity of the established order of things. So Burke was the master, but the master of many differing disciples when it came to the practical application of the general conservative view of man and society.

The Tories had, as we have seen, opposed parliamentary reform in 1832 but their severe losses in the first election under the reformed system had illustrated Burke's message that not all change was to be resisted, and that it might be better to support moderate reform rather than encourage extremism by opposing all change. General resistance might be doomed to failure; reaction almost certainly would be. The Tories became, in the wake of the 1832 Reform Act, the Conservatives and their approach to politics was illustrated by Peel's 'Tamworth Manifesto'[1] of 1835 in which, while attacking any radical proposals for reshaping society, he accepted the need for a moderate review of established institutions. Peel's non-reactionary form of conservatism, while meeting resistance in his party, established the possibility of an enduring role for a conservative party, and a permanent place for conservatism in modern British politics.

The major exponent of this aspect of conservatism which stressed a critique of society rather than a defence of the status quo was Samuel Taylor Coleridge (1772–1834). While he agreed with Burke as to the importance of land, and an aristocracy based on it, as one of the permanent features of a stable society, he also stressed the role of the professional and merchant classes as a progressive force to counterbalance the influence of land. Coleridge expected a harmony between the forces of order and those of progress; the threat of radical change only emerges when the ruling classes forget their duty, and this is the very thing that Coleridge saw happening in his own day. The industrial revolution had caused material advance but increased wretchedness and misery; in the pursuit of wealth, capitalism had destroyed and degraded; *laissez-faire* was the equivalent of that very neglect of duty which is likely to give rise to extremism. The conservative then in his indignation at the suffering of his fellow creatures has a duty to act on their behalf. Old institutions and old values should be preserved into the industrial age; far from changes being necessary to adjust to industrialism, it was industrialism that should adjust. So Coleridge, while sanctioning the traditional political structure, was quite prepared for it to be used to intervene in the economic field if duty so demanded. Far from parliament simply reflecting the country's dominant interests, it needed to react against some of those very interests. If the natural rulers of a society believed that intervention was necessary, no talk of freedom or *laissez-faire* was relevant. The idea of opposition between State and individual only existed on the assumption of the reality of individuals; if the group is dominant the individual should accept his subordinate role. The State is a moral unit, an organic whole, hierarchically organised, and as long as the rulers do not destroy their trust then harmony will prevail.

The conservative response to society for Coleridge then is not approval of whatever exists but harsh and vehement condemnation of all misery and wretchedness. The trading classes who have created this misery must be curbed; reform is necessary but it will be aris-

tocratic reform, not democratic. Thus, under Colderidge, conservatism carried its pre-industrial values into a new age, and by offering
a critique of industrialism managed to become a relevant and
progressive body of ideas. Its attack on industrialism was shared by
other groups, some representing those who actually suffered under
the system; where conservatism remained unique was in its emphasis
on the duty of the ruling classes as a necessary consequence of their
authority and privileged position in the social whole.

In addition to the State the constitution includes another institution, the National Church, whose commitment is to the maintenance and advancement of the moral life of the people. This
National Church or Clerisy comprised originally the learned in all
arts and sciences, including theology. Theology had a dominant role
because it contained within its compass the study of language,
history and philosophy. Thus the National Church, although distin-
guishable from the Christian Church, had historically become united
with it, and while the learned have in many areas separated from
the Clerisy, nevertheless the Clerisy still have a national role to play
and their rights and property must be protected. In the attack on the
evil consequences of industrialism, the Clerisy must ally itself with
the aristocracy in order to regulate the power of trade: while Coleridge stresses the virtue of traditional institutions, he demands that
they serve their proper purposes which are national and not narrowly
sectional. His is a critical conservatism where change, far from being
resisted, must sometimes be demanded; change, that is, which
forces society closer to the ideals developed through time.

The stress on membership of a social organism and duty to the
community also appears in the work of Matthew Arnold (1822–88)
who, like Coleridge before him and Disraeli after, opposed the
dominance of the idea of material and mechanical progress. He too
admired the notion of the aristocracy and believed that where it
remembered its duty and its position, as in England, it acted as a
stabilising and creative force, in contrast to countries like France
where in neglect of its duty it had helped to destroy traditional
French society. The aristocracy and the Church, as opposed to the
middle classes and the nonconformists, were the main civilising
forces in English society. However, not only were the classes
changing as the nineteenth century progressed – the aristocracy, for
example, were becoming materialistic – but the gulf between the
classes was becoming greater. For the social organism to regain its
health, unity must be recreated. Though he had little faith in mere
political reform, if a widened franchise offered the chance of

unifying the three classes then, despite the faults of the majority, it might offer hope for the future.

This idea of recreating a lost unity also appears prominently in the writings of the leading figure in nineteenth-century conservatism, Benjamin Disraeli (1804–81), who continued the tradition of conservatism as an adaptor of and to change rather than as a mere barrier to it. Disraeli began his career as a novelist, tried unsuccessfully to gain a seat in parliament, then joined the Tories and at last, on his fifth attempt, became a member in 1837. One of his earliest political works, the *Vindication of the English Constitution*,[2] expressed his basic position. As with Burke, he condemns the attempt to discover universal political principles; in committing this error the utilitarians take the same place for Disraeli as the French revolutionaries took for Burke. English politics, far from being a particular application of a universal theory, was a product of its history, and a study of its history would reveal the Whigs as an oligarchic self-interested class and the Tories as a national party, representing even if not elected by the whole people. Where the Whigs were represented as divisive, Disraeli offers the myth of national unity under the Tory party. Traditional institutions, when controlled by the Whigs, were used for party advantage; only the Tories would direct them responsibly, in the interest of the whole community. Disraeli thus provided political insight and popular sympathy for a party which not long before had appeared reactionary. Under Peel, it is true, the party had come to terms with change, but the change which it envisaged was change in response to middle-class demands. Disraeli, like Coleridge and Arnold, was more concerned with providing a genuine alternative to middle-class values, mainly materialistic and *laissez-faire*, and with offering a national role for a distinctive Tory party. This found expression in the Young England movement, a group of Tories disenchanted with the views and actions of Peel, whom they saw as limping from one reform to another without any consistent Tory rationale. In his novels of the 1840s[3] Disraeli expanded his analysis of English politics and society. The Tories under Peel had become a party without principles; unless it found a philosophy, a class-based democracy would defeat both it and the Whigs. Its purpose must be to restore authority and reverence in the community, a sense of duty to those with property, and a sense of unity between property and labour. To achieve this the aristocracy must live up to its responsibilities, the monarch must wield real power and the Church must pursue more energetically its spiritual mission. Such a re-invigorated traditional structure could hope to cope with the newer problems of class division arising out of industrialisation. The Tory party must attend to the social problems of irresponsible wealth and helpless poverty. The two nations, utterly foreign to each other, the one rich, the other poor, must be brought together. Before attempting this, and Disraeli did not specify the means, the party of conservatism must first be re-educated and revived. In addition to love of tradition and hierarchy, it must see the need for social equilibrium, through an emphasis on duty, as its main goal. In doing this it should ally itself with the people rather than fear them; the people have in common a love of tradition and hierarchy, as long as they have an organic role in the community, not an exploited one. Society would protect all if properly organised for mutual benefit, and this is possible in the industrial present as it was in the feudal past.

All this may be rather vague but it did establish paternalism and intervention as distinctive alternatives to traditional liberal theory, and it could do this because of its view of society as an organic whole with individuals as parts contributing to it, rather than as a collection of competing individuals. In this hierarchical society with its traditional institutions, social reform is a duty, and unity is the result. With such unity Disraeli believed that conservatism in England had a further purpose, that of consolidating and extending the Empire.[4]

At the beginning of the century the idea of Empire was being gradually eroded. America had been lost, Free Trade was threatening the system of protection, slavery was abolished in 1834; all factors weakening the strength of and the attachment to Empire. Yet Britain's imperial territories in the 1830s were worldwide. India, run at this time by the East India Company, was the greatest possession; there were Canada, Australia, the West Indies, Singapore, Malta and the Cape of Good Hope, as well as islands and posts scattered throughout the world. There were over a million Britons living overseas, including 56,000 soldiers garrisoned abroad,[5] yet there was little if any sense of an imperial mission. Originally Disraeli himself saw the colonies as millstones, and it was a view shared by many economists, if not by businessmen. Whatever the case, the Empire continued to grow but it only achieved a central place in British politics with Disraeli's adoption of imperialism as one of the major articles of the Conservative faith. It soon expressed a national sentiment, but while there were liberal and socialist imperialists, it was conservatism that was linked more closely with the idea, and that was to a large extent because of Disraeli's contribution. By the 1870s Burma, New Guinea, New Zealand, Natal and

Hong Kong had been acquired; with the development of an imperial enthusiasm large parts of Africa would before the end of the century also be added to the list. Despite the objections of liberals like Gladstone, imperialism became part of the English mentality and part of English conservatism. Along with social reform it was intended to unify the two nations and complete the vision of conservatism as a national ideology.

In concentrating on exponents of conservatism who stressed the need to incorporate change within traditional institutions it would be wrong to suggest that they met with no resistance from those who, on the contrary, saw change as something to be opposed. From Peel to Disraeli there was always a struggle for the dominance of the party; indeed, as we have seen, Disraeli himself was one of those who opposed Peel, and certainly Disraeli himself met sharp opposition. There was a continuing tradition within conservatism which criticised the path that history was taking, especially the democratic path of England. The 1832 Reform Act was bad enough; as we shall see, the 1867 Reform Act was even worse, and that was introduced by a Conservative administration. Writers like Thomas Carlyle who, like others, saw the evils of industrial society and the miseries and suffering of the working class, had no faith in that class itself solving its problems; leadership was of crucial importance and it should not be restrained by democratic control. It would be true to say that the dominant element in conservatism, as indeed in liberalism, was a suspicion, even a dread, of democracy rather than a Disraelian optimism that it could be brought under Tory control. In this Disraeli was in a minority and the party under Lord Salisbury, after Disraeli's death, reverted to a more resistant attitude to change. Salisbury saw the coming of democracy and the growth of social reform as threats to the power of Crown and aristocracy and as strengthening the class nature of political conflict. He stressed, as did many others within the conservative tradition, the dangers of democracy and the threat which the masses posed to the traditions which conservatism was pledged to defend.

On to the conservative tradition of respect for the past, a view of society as a hierarchical organism and a stress on duty rather than rights, two new features were grafted later in the nineteenth century, both arising from the split in the Liberal party over Ireland. The Unionists eventually joined with the Conservative party and brought with them two very different and opposing contributions. On the one hand Joseph Chamberlain offered a radical programme of social reform, demanding intervention by the State in favour of the disadvantaged. In the future he was to demand state activity in the field of tariff reform, seeking protection for imperial trade to replace the traditional free trade. This is not to say that his idea of interventionism was wholly successful within conservatism but it was something that could in principle be easily absorbed by a party committed to the paternalist duties of leadership. On the other hand, the Liberal split also led to some old-fashioned *laissez-faire* members joining the Conservatives, and this doctrinaire adherence, though mixing happily enough into the prejudice of much of conservatism, nevertheless lay uneasily within conservatism as a general view of society. However, with the growing threat from the rise of socialist ideas, conservatism did take on many similarities with the liberalism it had previously been concerned to oppose. Clearly conservatism had always accepted the importance of freedom, the rule of law, the protection of person and property and many other values in common with liberalism. But it had not regarded these as doctrinaire principles which should act as limits to parliamentary authority. The idea that there was an area of economic, or social, or indeed moral life into which the law should not in principle enter was alien to the view of society as an organism responsible for its own protection and growth. Though they might share a general hostility to government action this was never elevated into a principle.

These two aspects of interventionism and *laissez-faire* were both to contribute to the future tradition of conservatism[6] but in the nineteenth century the Liberal aspect based on individualism was a somewhat alien contribution to the organic Conservative view. What needs to be considered now is how far this general approach to society led to definite practical proposals for change. Unlike the Utilitarians or Liberals, the Conservative approach to reform was not based directly on principle but on a belief in the duty to provide a remedy whenever the community was suffering. Where action did take place – and it was often resisted if it threatened the dominance of land or property rights – it took place as a result of a sense of compassion, not out of a sense of injustice. It was duty that inspired reform, not a belief in rights. In seeing where that duty lay we shall notice that in the earlier part of the century the duty was perceived and acted on by individuals, and that it was only late in the century that the party collectively began to act from such considerations. As the State became the vehicle for social reform, the party accepted, though not unanimously, its national role in furthering such reform in a manner consistent with the traditions of an hierarchically organised society.

PRACTICAL PROPOSALS

Unlike other philosophies dealing with man and society, conservatism does not seek to develop practical programmes rigidly adhering to first principles. Rather, its practical proposals emerge in response to particular historical circumstances, and the general philosophy supplies limits within which to operate rather than first principles to act as logical starting points. Indeed the philosophy itself, as we have seen, generally becomes apparent through particular responses rather than being articulated in an abstract manner. The neatness of the utilitarian procedure from first principle to detailed application is not to be sought for in studying conservatism and its impact in the nineteenth century. Conservatism attacked the belief that society could be perfected by bringing into operation some abstract laws of human nature and the deductions therefrom. History was the proper context; to understand their practical perspective we must look to their responses, individually or collectively, to circumstances and events as they occurred through time. Thus, while their commitment to a paternalistic and responsible State lasted throughout the century, its base shifted from land and aristocracy at the beginning to a more national support at the end. Early Toryism was mainly an alliance of agrarian and traditional trading interests, with a commitment to ancient institutions at both central and local level. Thus they opposed parliamentary reform and local government changes where much of their power and patronage was exercised. Some went so far as to regard the constitution as so perfect as to require no change while others saw the need to conciliate the middle-class capitalists who were becoming conscious of their interests in opposition to those of land. It was never that simple, of course; many landowners became capitalists, and many capitalists became landowners, but there was no doubt as to the basic opposition arising between capital and land. This was exemplified by the Corn Law of 1815, designed to protect the interests of landowners by keeping foreign imports out and thus maintaining a high price at the expense of the consumers, increasingly urban, who in turn pressed their employers for higher wages. It was this alliance of the middle and working classes which increasingly pressed for parliamentary reform. The Tories reacted very much on class lines. Their repeal of the Test and Corporation Acts of 1828 and the Catholic Emancipation Act of 1829, which opened up the legislature and executive to non-Anglican Christians, showed that they were not rigidly hostile to all change, but here their class interest was not at stake. Parliamentary reform, however, seemed to threaten the dominance of the old world of property and patronage. While the Whigs, with very much the same interests, saw the need to accept change in order to maintain their aristocratic influence, the Tories fell from power because of their resistance to reform in 1832. Yet soon after, Peel was able to affirm at Tamworth the Conservative acceptance of political change, in particular the Reform Bill, as long as change was interpreted as a review of institutions, correction of abuses, redress of grievances, compatible with traditional rights and authority, rather than an instant reflection of any and all popular clamour. Despite opposition from within his own party, he succeeded in establishing cautious concession rather than rigid adherence to the old constitution as the dominant practical perspective of the new conservatism. It compromised with the middle classes despite opposition from both the reactionaries and the paternalist section of the party which favoured action for the distressed masses against the power of industrial capital. For this, Peel was to face Disraeli's criticism that he was conceding to middle-class pressure at the expense of holding any distinctively Conservative principles. The issue came to a head over the repeal of the Corn Laws, when the alliance of middle and working classes, temporarily established over Reform, re-established itself. For Peel protectionism had to go in the face of such a challenge, and the situation was made more urgent by the failure of the Irish potato crop and the likely famine resulting from it. Though Peel was convinced of the principle of Free Trade by this time, Ireland provided the occasion for action. As we shall see in the next section, Peel's measures were to split the party, with the Peelites for a time continuing independently and then some, like Gladstone, joining the Liberals, while the Protectionists with men like Disraeli eventually created what could be called a new Conservative party[7].

Despite Peel's dominance of the party up to 1846 and his belief that it must come to terms with the Industrial Revolution and the consequent power of manufacture and business, there remained in the party individual Conservatives of a more paternalistic outlook, who believed in duty as well as privilege and saw that duty as directing them to intervene on behalf of the workers and the poor. Over factory reform and the new Poor Law there seemed more in common between the working class and the landed aristocracy than between either and the middle class. This sense of responsibility for the lower classes drove men like Richard Oastler and Michael Sadler, in the 1830s, to expose factory conditions and press for a limitation of working hours. As early as 1802 there had been an attempt to regulate the hours and conditions of working children,[8] men like Robert Owen had shown the possibility of successfully combining efficiency with regulation,[9] and there had been other reform campaigns, though generally to little effect. Oastler began his campaign in 1830, drawing attention to the existence of 'child slavery' in Yorkshire. How could factory owners be prominent members of the anti-slavery movement and not see the slavery on their own doorsteps? Eventually Oastler was driven to campaign for a ten-hour day and, in alliance with working-class committees, agitated and organised. Soon this campaign spread to Lancashire and, in 1831, was taken into parliament by Michael Sadler, like Oastler a strongly religious and paternalistic Tory. Another figure in this same tradition soon joined the movement – Lord Ashley, later to become the most famous Tory reformer, the sixth Earl of Shaftesbury.

Thus while Peel was busy conciliating middle-class interests and moving his party away from reaction there was another tradition being kept alive, one critical of the consequences of the Industrial Revolution and opposed to the liberal view of unregulated competition. It attacked on a wide front: in addition to condemning factory conditions it also criticised the use of child and female labour in the mines, and attacked the evils of the new Poor Law. It urged an active Toryism where conscience was not simply to be paraded but to be acted upon. Disraeli's Young England movement and his later espousal of social reform, though less active than Oastler's, Sadler's or Ashley's version, was in the same tradition, and was one onto which Joseph Chamberlain's own radical programme could later be grafted. This tradition was not a necessary conclusion from an organic concept of society but was seen to be clearly consistent with it, and the sense of responsibility which lay behind paternalistic intervention was seen as morally obligatory.

With the Conservatives failing to gain a majority from 1846, when Peel split the party over the repeal of the Corn Laws, until 1874 (though with minority ministries in 1852, 1858–59 and 1866–68), and lacking the development of official party programmes, this tradition was mainly kept alive by individuals within the party rather than by the leadership itself. However, Disraeli's rise to the leadership offered the party a distinct philosophy and to some extent a practical programme. After the split with the Peelites, the Protectionists were left without a united policy and it was the task of Stanley, later the Earl of Derby, and Disraeli to unite the remnants of the party and give it a new direction. Derby's inclination was to accept progress and change but not to initiate it; to concede to widespread demand but to do nothing to create that demand. Disraeli's view was somewhat more positive – to ensure that change be consistent with tradition rather than carried out in response to abstract principle or general doctrine. The crucial issue they had to face was that of parliamentary reform. They had made an unsuccessful attempt to deal with this in 1859; in 1866 Gladstone introduced his Reform Bill, which was defeated by Conservatives and right-wing Liberal opposition. Could Derby and Disraeli remain content with this victory, or would it identify the party with that very resistance to change which they were concerned to oppose? For whatever particular reasons – and we shall examine these in more detail in the next section – Derby and Disraeli passed, in 1867, a more extreme Reform Bill than the defeated Liberal one, thus establishing the alliance of Toryism and reform which was to be Disraeli's greatest contribution to Conservatism. Once political reform had taken place he believed that the urgent priorities were social; in his Crystal Palace speech[10] he described the most important problem, that of the health of the community, in these words:

> It is a large subject. It has many branches. It involves the state of dwellings of the people, the moral consequences of which are not less considerable than the physical. It involves their enjoyment of some of the chief elements of nature – air, light and water. It involves the regulation of their industry, the inspection of their toil. It involves the purity of their provisions and it touches upon all the means by which you may wean them from habits of excess and of brutality.

In combination with his defence of traditional institutions and his espousal of the imperialistic cause, this gave conservatism if not a political programme, at least a practical dimension which distinguished it from liberalism. What followed from this commitment to the 'condition of the people' question remains to be seen; at the very least it favoured intervention in social policy – in matters of health, industrial conditions and housing – in opposition to the *laissez-faire* still favoured by many of the middle classes. Disraeli's popular sympathies, which led him to extend the franchise and favour social reform or, on a more cynical view held by many at the time, his unprincipled gamble with the future of his party, led to success. From a party which in 1868 was still mainly county and agricultural it moved to being a party in 1855 which owed half its support to urban constituencies. Policy alone, of course, did not account for this; in 1867 the National Union of Conservative and Constitutional Associations was formed and in 1870 the Conservative Central Office was founded, designed to attract, organise and mobilise support as an alternative to traditional means now irrelevant to a new political and social context.[11]

There is a danger in overstressing the changes that any individual, be it a Peel or a Disraeli, succeeded in bringing about in the nature of conservatism. The 'progressive' elements were always resisted by those who saw such changes as undesirable, and the party has always seen a tension between these two forces. Disraeli's own position was constantly assailed,[12] though his successful defence of his position allowed the 'progressive' image to dominate and bring about in 1885 almost twenty years of only briefly interrupted Conservative rule. Disraeli's ministry of 1874–80, which saw more social measures passed than by any other single government in the century, firmly established the tradition of intervention as being one of the acceptable Conservative responses to social problems. How far this intervention was a necessary result of conservatism, or simply consistent with it, as one choice amongst others, we must consider in the next section; whatever the relationship, interventionism was seen at the time, and since, as being central to Disraelian conservatism as a practical perspective.

This tradition was continued by Lord Randolph Churchill and his Tory democracy and later by Joseph Chamberlain after he had left the Liberals over Home Rule for Ireland. Before we look at their practical contributions, however, it is important to note that the rival tradition within conservatism was not without life and vigour. Lord Salisbury (1830–1903), who was Disraeli's successor in the Lords while Sir Stafford Northcote led the Commons (there was no machinery for choosing an overall leader while in opposition) and who became Prime Minister in 1885–86, 1886–92 and 1895–1902, began his career as an opponent of Disraeli, resigning over the 1867 Reform Act. He believed that democracy was dangerous to liberty and property and that in its likely attack on inequality it would endanger national prosperity and stability. The Conservative view depended on the importance of an unequal society and he saw the attempt to gain working-class support through social reform as opportunist bribery. While not opposed to all change he was pessimistic about its results; he certainly opposed the easy assumption that for every political problem there is a solution, and that thus through vigorous government action there will be a reduction in the total number of problems. Yet he was no narrow reactionary; he believed that the Conservative cause must be defended by appealing to instincts shared by all classes, and to this end he accepted the practical need to integrate the working classes into the social whole by reforming their living conditions. While sceptical about the role of central authority in general, he accepted its intervention over particular problems; there was no doctrinaire opposition to intervention, merely a suspicion as to its dangers if it began to threaten liberty and property. Thus where the Disraelian alliance was forged with the working classes, Salisbury appealed much more to those sections of the middle class disillusioned with the radical tenor of Liberalism and later with its plans for Home Rule for Ireland. Property and inequality, once the cry of the aristocracy, now appealed too to the middle classes in the face of a rising working class. Thus Salisbury was enabled to slow down the pace of social legislation without losing electoral support. In his concern to maintain the support of traditional Conservatives and in his dislike of electoral bribery, he managed nevertheless to create new support. In his resistance to Churchill and Chamberlain he gained large middle-class support which, in its hostility to Liberal radicalism, could turn to a party which managed to keep its radicals in check.

Although Salisbury dominated the party for over twenty years he, like others before him, met resistance, this time from those who were concerned to keep alive the Disraelian heritage. The Fourth Party (the other three being the two major parties and the Irish) consisted of Lord Randolph Churchill, Arthur Balfour, Sir Henry Drummond Wolff and J. E. Gorst, and was in some ways similar to Disraeli's Young England movement of the 1840s. Their main campaign in the Commons was waged against their own party under Northcote, as much as against Gladstone. Their politics were radical if vague and somewhat incoherent, and their main battleground was the party organisation. The National Union had been founded in 1867 and Gorst had been involved in it from the beginning, in addition to having been party agent in the 1870s. His concern was with urban conservatism and with developing an organisation and propaganda to appeal to the new voters rather than relying on the older methods of influence, patronage and corruption. The Secret Ballot Act of 1872 and the Corrupt Practices Act of 1883 made such a change more necessary and urgent. The National Union came to be seen not only as a means of organising local Conservative Associations but also as a means by which those associations could influence the party. This was one sense of the term 'Tory democracy', which co-existed with the older sense of paternalistic social reform, though at times the term also seems to have meant little more than a democracy ruled over by Tories. As a result the National Union could come into conflict with the party leadership, and the Fourth Party made sure that it did, though Churchill may well have been using this conflict for reasons of personal political ambition, involving the destruction of Northcote's leadership in the Commons. The conflict between the increasingly middle-class National Union and the party's Central Committee appeared to be about democracy, though in reality there was no serious challenge to the leadership's right to decide policy; the major concern was that the organisational needs of the party were inefficiently pursued by the Central Committee, dominated by the Whigs. Though Gorst was genuinely concerned with party organisation and capturing electoral support, Churchill led the conflict over such details as a vehicle for his own career. Though he talked of democracy and the working classes, in the tradition of Disraeli, his attempts at power seemed to have been motivated more by his personal ambition than by his commitment to politics. Though Salisbury ended the conflict by ending the Central Committee, the balance of power between party leadership and National Union remained as before. There was never any serious attempt to mirror the National Liberal Federation, committed to policy as well as organisation; thus Churchill's challenge to the leadership was ultimately shallow – it might bring success against a Northcote but was doomed to failure against a Salisbury. Apart from keeping alive the rhetoric of Tory social reform, Churchill achieved little else but to strengthen middle-class activity in the urban constituencies – that very class least likely to embrace the tradition he was vaguely and incoherently upholding.

The agreement eventually reached between Salisbury and Churchill came just in time to decide on the appropriate response to Gladstone's 1884 Reform Bill proposing household suffrage in the counties. As might be expected, some Conservatives favoured outright opposition while others saw the need to amend the proposals in such a way as to minimise their radical effects. The solution was to concentrate not on electoral suffrage but on the redistribution of seats, so that Tories would not be swamped by Liberals and radicals in multi-member constituencies. The effect of the redistribution proposals was that Tories were protected by dividing up many old constituencies into single member ones. The election in 1885 gave the Irish the balance of power. Gladstone was defeated over Home Rule in 1886, following an electoral agreement between the Conservatives and Liberal Unionists and the result was a large

Unionist majority. The importance of this for Conservatism was the secession from the Liberals both of the old Whigs previously tied to the party by family tradition rather than ideological commitment, and a number of radicals led by Joseph Chamberlain.

Chamberlain (1836–1914) was a much more substantial figure than Churchill, though no doubt Chamberlain's belief that his radicalism could find a place within Conservatism owed much to Churchill's critical activities within his party. Although it was Unionism over Ireland which enabled an alliance to be formed between the Conservatives and the radicals, Chamberlain saw his role as giving conventional Conservatism a radical dimension. His 'unauthorised programme' was not abandoned; though he rejected the idea of a Cabinet combination in 1886, he believed in the possibility of influence over the Cabinet by the Radical Unionists. He opposed the negative policy both of the Whig Unionists and of traditional Conservatives; his unionism was not to override his radicalism. Social and political reform must be pushed forward, partly to satisfy legitimate demand and partly to undermine Liberal support. Many of his old schemes were still advanced despite much opposition: the giving of compulsory powers to local authorities to purchase land for allotments, the regulation of conditions of work of merchant seamen, the extension of local government democracy to the counties on the lines of municipal institutions, free education, public works, land purchase and county government in Ireland, and giving rural labourers help to buy smallholdings. His attitude was still that expressed before his final split with the Liberals, and can be summed up in the words of the editor of *The Radical Programme*, published in 1885. Referring to radical proposals, he had this to say, with Chamberlain's approval:[13]

> They sound the death-knell of the *laissez-faire* system . . . The goal towards which the advance will probably be made at an accelerated pace is that in the direction of which the legislation of the last quarter of a century has been tending – the intervention, in other words, of the State on behalf of the weak against the strong, in the interests of labour against capital, of want and suffering against luxury and ease.

Clearly this was not acceptable either to his Whig allies or to Conservatives; when in 1892 he urged Salisbury to accept a positive policy of social legislation as being in harmony with Conservative tradition, Salisbury's reaction was to see the danger of splitting the party and to assert the folly of initiating any changes which might lead to such a result. Although Salisbury was Prime Minister of a government which passed a great deal of social legislation up to 1892, he was reluctant to see these changes as systematic rather than as individual responses to social ills. He preferred to keep the alliance together on the basis of opposition to Home Rule rather than to adopt a general programme of social reform; this was due to a traditional prejudice against centralisation as much as to a hostility to doctrinaire commitment.

Chamberlain's other contribution to conservatism in this period was his imperialism, again something which had set him apart from Gladstonian Liberalism. His commitment originated in his belief that the Empire would help solve domestic problems of unemployment and finance social reform, but it soon became a belief in the greatness of the Empire itself. In 1895, when Salisbury returned to power after three years of Liberal government, the Liberal Unionists joined the cabinet, and it was the Colonial Office which Chamberlain decided to accept. This encouragement of imperialism appealed to the middle classes very much, as his support of social reform appealed to the working classes. Chamberlain's glorification of the Empire, as with his programme of social reform, went much further than Disraeli's; he believed that keeping the Empire strong demanded state action on an economic as well as a military and diplomatic level. Protective tariffs to support imperial industry against European and American competition would not only unite the Empire and protect British industry but also provide a means of financing social reform without taxing the property of the middle and landed classes. In this he was opposed not only by fellow Unionists but by Liberal supporters of Free Trade who, though they supported social reform, believed in financing it by direct taxation rather than by tariffs on foreign imports. Chamberlain resigned from office in 1903 in order to campaign for tariff reform, a cause which eventually captured the party but only after a huge Liberal victory in 1906, and after many Conservative defections.

As we have already pointed out, it was not only the interventionist and imperialist element, represented by Chamberlain, which was absorbed by Conservatism as a result of the Liberal split; the old Whigs also joined and in combination with increasing middle-class support this reinforced the other tradition in Conservatism, a hostility to change and intervention. From this time Conservatism had to make room for the old-fashioned 'liberal' commitment to the free market, based not just on traditional conservative hostility to change but also on a more positive, more doctrinaire belief in the virtues of the market and in individual initiative and free enterprise.

While those elements which were concerned to absorb change in a manner consistent with tradition became increasingly interventionist, those elements concerned to oppose change became increasingly 'liberal' in the sense that they came to include in their picture of society a view of the free market previously seen as in opposition to the more paternalistic Conservative view of the relationship between classes. As the official Liberals were to become influenced by New Liberalism, which also sanctioned state intervention, and were eventually to almost disappear from the scene, the defence of the free enterprise, competitive system found its home amongst a Conservative party previously unsaddled by such doctrinaire commitment. Though Peel's acceptance of the demands of the middle classes had been rejected by the Conservatives in 1846 it was to become more and more a feature of conservatism after 1885, in tension with, if not dominating over, the Disraelian heritage. This is not to claim, of course, that such hostility to state intervention had not been present before. As we shall see when we examine Disraeli's reforming administration, there were always elements opposed to the use of the State in economic and social matters; what was new was the conversion of this prejudice against state involvement into doctrine.

IMPACT ON LEGISLATION

As we have seen, the Tories under Wellington opposed the reform of the House of Commons in 1832 but then under Peel adopted a policy of cautious moderation rather than outright reaction. Apart from a brief period in office in 1834 they were out of power until 1841, when Peel formed his government which was to last until the party broke up over the repeal of the Corn Laws in 1846. Peel's basic position in office, as in opposition, was to admit the political and economic power of the middle classes and to persuade the Conservative party to recognise this new situation In this desire to accommodate middle-class interests Peel adopted their view that the main target of government should be a healthy economy and that this could be best achieved without government intervention. However, as we have seen already, there was at the same time within conservatism an attitude critical of the consequences of industrialisation and this demanded government intervention and an end to unregulated competition. Based on a paternalist view of society, it elevated duty above self-interest, or at least the duty of the ruling class above the self-interest of the middle classes. Although this view did not dominate the party, the actions of individuals like Oastler in organising agitation over factory conditions and like Sadler and Ashley in taking the campaign to parliament, were of great influence. In creating a campaign, in mobilising support and in forming an alliance with working-class opposition to factory conditions, these Tories helped create the climate for legislation. Though the Utilitarians of the period were influential in determining the type of intervention finally adopted, it was Conservatives like Oastler outside parliament and Sadler and Ashley within who built up the pressures and demands to act at all in the face of middle-class opposition.

Such paternalistic and interventionist sympathy with the working class was not, however, the main Conservative response. Peel's attitude was one of co-operation with Whigs and resistance to radicals, whether liberal or Tory. Thus he supported the extension of reform to municipal corporations in 1835, and defended the position of the Church in matters of finance and its role in education, opposing plans for the abolition of church rates and the introduction of secular education. Peelite Conservatism, while defending the traditional position of the monarchy, the House of Lords and the Church, at the same time attempted to bring in to the Conservative fold the newer professional and industrial classes. The defence of land as a Tory priority was presented as compatible with the defence of industry and commerce, and this strategy brought Peel success in 1841.

His administration coincided with two of the greatest extra-parliamentary movements of the century – Chartism and the Anti-Corn Law League. In the case of Chartism, disillusion with the 1832 Reform Act, coupled with their experience of the Whig government, led working-class radicals to believe that nothing less than radical reform leading to a change of rulers would improve the social and economic position of the working classes. The Whigs had opposed further parliamentary reform and the Ten Hour Movement, they were opposed to trade unions and had brought in the Poor Law Amendment Act which, to working-class eyes, established poverty as a crime to be punished by misery and degradation. Political reform was seen as essential to social improvement; universal suffrage was the road to emancipation.

The Anti-Corn Law League was given a similar impetus by the failure of the reformed parliament. Their disillusion was more understandable than was that of the Chartists; the recognition of industrial and commercial interests in the Reform Act had led many to hope for reform along middle-class lines. Of course, in the case of the Corn Laws such reform would threaten the interest of land, and the reformed parliament was still very much a representative of land with limited scope for manufacture and business. Thus middle-class reformers felt, as the Chartists did, that pressure for change must come from without. Both movements were strengthened by the economic depression of the late 1830s which helped transform the organisations into popular movements. The economic crisis made more urgent the demands which both groups were urging; their activities represented, and in turn strengthened, a newly emerging class consciousness. How did Peel cope with such pressures in the period 1841–46? Indeed, would he be able to cope as leader of a party committed to the constitution, Church and landed property?

Strategically, Peel believed in satisfying the middle classes and in improving the economy so that the position of the working classes would be bettered without the necessity for direct intervention. His budget of 1842 and then of 1845 relaxed restrictions on trade, reduced protection and reintroduced income tax. Though it did pass a Mines Act in 1842 and a Factory Act in 1844, the government's main aim was increasingly the liberalisation of trade. Where intervention in industry was allowed this was in response to the activities of individuals rather than a result of government initiative. The Mines Act introduced by Ashley was a much weakened version of his original bill, and one passed despite lack of active government support. It made illegal the employment of females, male children under ten and those under fifteen where machines were worked; to supervise these restrictions the Home Secretary was given power to appoint inspectors. Ashley was to be similarly disappointed over the Factory Act of 1844, which fell short of his goal of a ten-hour day. It did reduce the work of children over nine to six and a half hours and the working day of females was reduced to twelve hours; also inspectors were given supervisory powers. In both cases, however, the power of industry (not just the middle-class industrialists; as many coal owners were landed aristocrats) diluted the original proposals in a way that would have been extremely difficult had Peel thrown his support behind them. However, his approach to social questions was becoming increasingly 'liberal' as opposed to paternalist; his final stage on this road was his adoption of Free Trade and the destruction of protectionism. He had been reducing the tariff on imported food – cattle, wheat, corn, sugar – from 1842 on, and in 1846 he proposed his final act of economic liberalism – the repeal of the Corn Laws. Although extra-parliamentary agitation for this was widespread, Peel seems to have acted out of conviction rather than expediency; how else could his destruction of the Conservative party for the sake of Free Trade be explained?

The summer of 1845 saw extremely bad harvests, and in Ireland the reasonable grain crop was exported to England, leaving the Irish to eat what was left of a disastrously infected potato crop. The widespread famine which resulted could not be met through the public works and private charity which came into operation; something more drastic was needed and Peel determined to repeal the Corn Laws, though that was unlikely to have any immediate effect. Unable to carry his protectionist colleagues, Peel resigned in 1845 but took up office again when Lord John Russell, now converted to the Repeal cause, declined to form a government and risk splitting the Whig party. In 1846 Peel put forward his comprehensive proposals: the abolition or reduction of duties on many manufactured goods, the reduction of the duty on many imported foods and its abolition on all others except corn and livestock. Eventually protection was to disappear on all grains; to compensate landed interests the laws of settlement were to be amended so that paupers would no longer be returned from towns to home parishes, the government was to subsidise medical and educational services under the poor law, and in other ways remove the burden from local rates. The Corn and Customs Bills were passed in 1846 to great acclaim in the country, but the protectionists under the future Lord Derby, Lord George Bentinck and Disraeli, allied with the Whigs and with the Irish to vote Peel out of office. His belief in the necessity for change in order to preserve, and for accommodation with the new forms of property arising in the nineteenth century was rejected by those who, for the time at least, preferred to resist rather than assimilate the demands of the new industrial age.

This disaster and the departure from the party of the Peelites placed Disraeli in a prominent position, soon that of leader of the party in the House of Commons. How would his view of Toryism as the party of social improvement fit in with the reactionary role it had just played over the Corn Laws? Could the party which had so emphatically defended the landed interest fulfil the role of leadership and unite the two nations in the required hierarchical and paternalistic manner? Had Disraeli's concern for social reform been less vague and unsystematic and more concrete and detailed his task would have been extremely difficult, given the general view of his party. As it was Disraeli shared many of the prejudices of his party and held social improvement more as an ideal than as a programme. Thus he opposed the Public Health Act of 1848 as being too centralist, opposed the Mines Bill of 1850 which would have provided for inspection, and yet supported the Ten-Hour cause. Where Conservative commitment to local autonomy and property were not involved he was prepared to support state intervention; where they were involved his attitude tended to be negative though not reactionary. Part of this is no doubt explained by his recognition that the party must be drawn slowly away from its reactionary inclinations towards a more progressive stance, but part also is to be explained by the doubts he shared with the rest of his party regarding increased centralisation and diminution of local independence. With the secession of the Peelites the party was more than ever the party of the counties where local autonomy was highly valued; it was not only talent that was lost to the party when the Peelites left but also a balance between county and municipal borough. Derby's brief minority government in 1852 and Disraeli's budget of that year reflected these two points: the government was referred to as the 'Who? Who?' ministry, and the budget strongly favoured the agricultural industry at the expense of the towns.

From 1855 to 1865, a decade in which Palmerston dominated the scene, the Conservative party was left to support his domestic policy and do little more than hope that after him their chance might come. Another brief ministry in 1858–59 revealed little that was distinctly Conservative but, after Palmerston's death in 1865, their chance did come over the issue of Reform. After this was settled the party was again to take on a distinctive character and to do so successfully, gaining electoral support from the middle and working classes and escaping from its narrower rural base. Gladstone introduced his Reform Bill in 1866 and a combination of right-wingers within the Liberal party and the Conservative opposition defeated it, leading to the government's resignation and a minority Conservative government. This government under Derby and Disraeli then passed a Reform Act in 1867 more radical than the Liberal Bill rejected the year before. Thus the brief details; let us look more closely at the events in question. The first point to note is that neither Derby nor Disraeli were opposed to Reform in principle; not only was there a demand for it but it was their role as leaders of a Conservative party to ensure that change, when it came, should be made compatible both with the traditions of the country and with the fortunes of their own party. They were also aware that a wider extension of the suffrage might help their party more than a minor extension. So it is not a change of principle that needs explanation; rather a change of strategy or tactics, either willingly accepted or forced on them. On one explanation Reform is seen as consistent with Disraeli's old views regarding the alliance of interest between the landed aristocracy and the industrial working class. Thus the extension of the franchise was meant to establish a democracy under Tory control, and Disraeli is credited with foreseeing the eventual support which a large section of the working classes were to give to the Conservative party. Against this interpretation lies the evidence that much of the Reform Act was a reaction to the pressures of the time and that Derby and Disraeli went further than originally intended. This pressure was of different sorts: extra-parliamentary working-class agitation, parliamentary amendments threatening to a minority government and the realities of the distribution of electoral support.

In 1866 there was strong working-class agitation for reform culminating in the mass demonstration in Hyde Park in 1867 organised by the Reform League. This was not just a response to economic crisis or a demand for the vote; it was as much a defence of the crucial working-class institutions, the trade unions. The growing strength of unions was feared on account of the challenge they represented both to orthodox economic theory and to established forms of power. Their legal position had never been entirely clear; since 1825 they had ceased to be unlawful but their actions were often interpreted by the courts as such; since 1855 registration as Friendly Societies seemed to give them legal status and protection but a legal judgment of 1867 denied them this. While the Conservatives were not prepared to legislate and make unions completely legal – they set up a Royal Commission instead – the government was concerned to conciliate in ways short of this. The extension of the suffrage to satisfy vigorous working-class demand was seen as less dangerous than submitting to the larger demand of legitimising trade union power.

It is also clear that the government was never in full control of the passage of the Reform Bill, and many amendments extending the franchise were passed without any consistent Conservative reaction to them. Once Disraeli had accepted Reform there seemed to be no firm principles determining its detail, and thus the final version was to some extent a reflection of the varying pressures exerted in the House. Of course the one virtue this did have was that the final Bill, whatever its content, would be one identified with a Conservative government: after so long in opposition this was no mean achievement. Further, the fact that it was a Conservative Bill gave Derby and Disraeli more control over the redistribution of seats, which benefited their own party. The final version established household suffrage for boroughs and this was to act as the basic principle (it was extended to counties in 1885) until 1918, and as we have seen it did seem to go further than might be expected from a party still tied to the land. However, one point needs noting to place this Reform in a perspective where it becomes less of a puzzle and that is the brief record of this administration before it introduced its Reform Bill. There again we see little definite plan and yet not insubstantial achievement. Although little was done in the field of labour or mining, it did increase regulation of factory employment by extending existing Acts to more trades and manufactures,[14] and by bringing in new regulations in smaller establishments employing less than 100 persons.[15] However, the Conservative preference for local rather than central power emerged in the responsibility for enforcement in smaller establishments going to the local authorities and not to central factory inspectors. Regulation was extended even into the area of agricultural labour; similarly with merchant shipping. In the area of the sick poor the government abandoned the Poor Law principles of deterrence and local control. The Metropolitan Poor Act of 1867, which freed the sick from the poorhouse, was a recognition of the State's responsibility to set up a system of medical care for the poor, a system which was gradually extended throughout the country. The Public Health Bill, though introduced by the Liberal ministry, was passed by the Conservatives in a much stronger form, imposing duties and central compulsion. In the field of working-class housing the government looked favourably on a Bill to allow local authorities to demand improvement on condemned housing and, when not done, to clear and build.

Although such improvements were limited they do show the willingness of Conservatives at the time to accept new methods, especially state interference in social matters, and to come to terms with the new economic situation. What they refused to see in 1846 they saw now more clearly than many Liberals. Thus the Reform Act of 1867 was not such a trauma as might have been expected, though Gladstone's victory in the subsequent election lent support to Disraeli's critics that not only was he an unprincipled gambler but, even worse, an unsuccessful one. Now that Conservatism had come to terms with its new role, even inaugurated a new era, would it suffer the irony of rejection by the forces it had brought into electoral being?

In 1874 Disraeli won a sweeping victory and formed the first majority Conservative government for nearly thirty years. How would Disraelian Conservatism work in practice? There is little disagreement that this administration saw the greatest era of active social legislation in the century. However, there is dispute as to whether this was an application of ideas already formed and thus a consistent programme in response to Conservative ideology, or whether the period is better seen as a disjointed series of reactions to circumstances with ideology having little impact. As we have seen, a similar debate occurs around the question of Benthamite influence in the early part of the century – did governments act in response to ideas or because the situation had become intolerable? In the case of Disraeli the view has been put forward that, far from there having been a coherent policy, legislation was largely dictated by the pressures of immediate circumstances. On this interpretation there was no 'policy',simply 'empiricism tempered by prejudice'.[16] Of course, just as views of what is intolerable change with changing values, and ideas play a role in shaping these values, so the 'prejudice' which tempers 'empiricism' also changes – the prejudice of a Disraeli will be different from that of a Peel, and this is bound to affect the interpretation given to circumstances as well as the subsequent reaction. Thus the 'empiricism' does not exist apart from the 'prejudice'; whether 'the facts' are seen as problems needing solutions, and what kind of solutions are appropriate, is dependent on the cluster of ideas, the prejudice if you like, in this case what we call Disraelian Conservatism. Although it is true that no programme was deduced in detail on the basis of Conservative principles, nevertheless Disraeli's Conservative perspective indicated and limited the kinds of response available. Thus absence of a master plan does not indicate an absence of coherence. So, although it can be argued that Disraeli's career was primarily that of a superb opportunist, yet his very success in that direction relied on his ability to utilise ideas, and these ideas in turn limited or modified what was considered acceptable. If we look now at some of the main reforms that took place we shall see that they reflect the main priorities of Disraeli's vision of conservatism, modified by the more reactionary influence of the newer middle-class adherents to the Conservative party, who brought with them their liberal commitments to the free market to strengthen the Peelite tradition of an alliance between landed and industrial and commercial property. It was in this conflict between the paternalist organic view of society and the individualist view that Disraeli's supervision of and general approval for social reform were crucial. Though himself not an active reformer, his leadership allowed the tradition of social improvement to survive fairly successfully despite objections from liberal and reactionary conservatives.

In 1874 the government passed its Factory Act which abolished full-time employment below the age of fourteen, half-time employment below the age of ten and imposed the maximum of fifty-six and a half hours for women and children in the textile industry. Though adult males were not limited in law they would be in practice given the importance of women and children in textile production. In the next year the Employers and Workmen Bill (to replace the Master and Servant Act) and the Conspiracy and Protection of Property Bill gave trade unionism much of what it demanded: the first stopped breaches of contract from being criminal acts unless life or property or vital public services were threatened, and the second allowed collective bargaining and the right to strike. Later that year peaceful picketing was made legal. Between them these various Acts were intended to remove industrial conflict through recognition of the rights of labour, and to establish Disraeli's belief that the working classes had more to hope for from Conservatives than from Liberals – a neat mixture of genuine belief in social reform with a calculation of electoral advantage, two consistent Disraelian priorities.

In 1875 attempts were made to deal with the problem of working-class housing and public health. The Artisans Dwelling Bill enabled authorities in the larger towns to improve districts certified as unhealthy by purchasing land, compulsorily if necessary, and letting or selling it for working-class housing, to be erected by private industry. Those families displaced by such schemes were to be rehoused in or near the same area. Money was to be lent cheaply from public funds to finance such purchase. Although the powers under this Bill were permissive rather than compulsory, it did embody a striking blow to those adherents of the free market who criticised its compulsory purchase clauses and its cheap loans provision. In its attempt to tackle the problem of working-class housing it placed social improvement of the necessities of life above the rights of property; though its applications relied on local initiative it nevertheless asserted the responsibility of government in a relatively new area. In an older area of government action the Public Health Act of 1875 consolidated and improved many older sanitary laws; the Sale of Food and Drugs Act proscribed adulteration, though without insisting on the appointment of analysts who might make it effective; the Pollution of Rivers Act, though mild, did express a desire to improve the general health of the community in line with Disraeli's general beliefs. All these various acts asserted a paternalist belief in social reform but held back from too vigorous an application in the face of liberal conservative opposition.

A similar tension between paternalist intervention and a reluctance to enlarge the responsibility of the State can be seen in the Friendly Societies Act 1875 and the Merchant Shipping Act 1876. The Friendly Societies had millions of small savers concerned with providing for themselves in sickness and old age, but there was no safeguard against incompetence or dishonesty through either compulsory registration or auditing. The government in this case did very little beyond giving information to and collecting information from the societies; it refused to interfere further by imposing any restrictions on the societies beyond limiting the amount that infants could be insured for. Paternalism here was not strong enough to dominate the middle-class hostility to intervention. Nor was it in the field of merchant shipping where, though safety demanded regulation and inspection, the government declined to go beyond the enforcement of liability to the adoption of strict government regulation.

In the field of education too compulsion was avoided, though a measure of indirect compulsion was accepted. Parents were not forced to send their children to school but there were certain penalties if they did not. Children between ten and fourteen could not work if they had not attended school or reached a certain educational standard, unless they continued school half-time under the Factory Acts or local bye-laws. Children who did well at the age of ten were to be offered free education for the next three years, and the government raised its contributions to the voluntary schools, thus strengthening their position in their rivalry with the school boards. Although the measure indicated a desire for general elementary education, it retained the belief in voluntarism and in the role of the Church and its landed patrons. Nevertheless it did carry education further than had the Liberals' 1870 Act.

Thus what we have called Disraelian Conservatism – the commitment to social improvement – though it determined the course of legislative action in this period, was never unchallengeably dominant and the reactionary and liberal strands in Conservatism were always present, opposing legislation, each for its own reasons. Towards the end of his ministry, Disraeli and the government generally gave more and more attention to foreign affairs and the Empire, and less and less to domestic issues. The election of 1880 led to defeat and a further strengthening of those elements determined to resist change and limit the sphere of government. The interest in the condition of the people declined until re-awakened by the radical Joseph Chamberlain – ironically enough, the very man whose policies had helped strengthen the Conservative party by alarming sections of the middle classes. However, though this interest was henceforth to be regarded as a legitimate influence, due to the Disraelian heritage, it was to be subordinate for the rest of the century to the very different Conservatism represented by Lord Salisbury.

In 1881 Salisbury succeeded Disraeli, then the Earl of Beaconsfield, as leader of the party in the Lords, with Sir Stafford Northcote as leader in the Commons. He became Prime Minister in 1885, then from 1886 to 1892, and again from 1895 to 1902. During this time he saw his role as one of restraining the efforts – which were rather vague – of Lord Randolph Churchill and – more vigorous and detailed – of Joseph Chamberlain, both directed towards a policy of social legislation. Thus although his administrations passed a good deal of such legislation, partly as we shall see, under pressure from Chamberlain and his Radical Unionists, yet he was reluctant to have this seen as an important part of the Conservative approach. Where Disraeli or Chamberlain were happy to elevate social reform into the forefront of Conservative philosophy, Salisbury was concerned that it be seen as a justified response to individual problems rather than a general inclination to use the State to improve society. While he was conscious of the paternalist duties of ruling, and thus could accept state intervention, he was also aware of the importance of liberty and property and thus refused to accept intervention as a general policy. Chamberlain, on the other hand, until he entered the Cabinet in 1895 as Colonial Secretary, when the Empire and later tariff reform dominated his energies, maintained his radical commitment to social reform, and his influence on Salisbury's government was important.

In 1888 the government passed a Local Government Act extending democratic control to counties on the same lines as municipalities; in 1891 it made primary education free in both board and denominational schools; in 1892 it passed a Small Holdings Act to help the labourer buy land, an attempt to restore peasant proprietorship in a way that had not been achieved by the Allotment Act of 1887. All these were part of the radical 'unauthorised programme' and in all these the influence of the Radical Unionists was, if not decisive, yet clearly important. On the other hand the government was more prepared to intervene than Salisbury's views might suggest. It passed legislation intended to improve working-class housing and public health,[17] it established inspection of factories where only adult males were employed,[18] it regulated shop hours,[19] and encouraged technical and intermediate education.[20] So the old Tory paternalism was not entirely swamped by middle-class liberal adherents and in many ways could marry quite easily with the radicalism of a Chamberlain. However, in Salisbury's last administration very little was done in the field of social conditions, though this was as much due to concern with Britain's foreign and imperial position as to hostility to state activity. Even Chamberlain by this time was putting the Empire and the world first, as Disraeli had done and Salisbury was also doing; social reform might have divided Conservatives but they remained united that, important or not, it had to take second place if it clashed with a greater Conservative good, the position of Britain in the world. From then on Salisbury's concern with Britain's foreign policy, and Chamberlain's with Imperial Protection, left the area of social reform to the Liberals who, when they regained power in 1906, were to be committed to social change and to New Liberalism.

REFERENCES AND NOTES

1. An extract appears in the collection, useful despite the omission of Coleridge, edited by Buck, P. W. (1975) *How Conservatives Think*. Penguin: Harmondsworth

2. Collected with other of his theoretical writings in *Whigs and Whiggism: Political Writings by Benjamin Disraeli* (1913) ed. Hutcheon, W. Murray: London

3. *Coningsby* (1844) and *Sybil* (1845), subtitled respectively *The New Generation* and *The Two Nations* republished *Coningsby* (1959) Dent: London and *Sybil* (1954) Penguin: Harmondsworth

4. Speech at the Banquet of the National Union of Conservative and Constitutional Associations, 24 June 1872

5. From p. 27 of the first volume *Heaven's Command* in that superb trilogy by James Morris (1979) *An Imperial Progress*. Penguin: Harmondsworth

6. W. H. Greenleaf (1973) 'The Character of Modern Conservatism' in *Knowledge and Belief in Politics*, (ed. Benewick, R., Berki, R. N. and Parekh, B.). Allen and Unwin: London

7. This is argued in Blake, R. (1972) *The Conservative Party from Peel to Churchill*, chapter II. Fontana: London
8. Introduced by Sir Robert Peel, father of the future Prime Minister
9. Owen was an extremely successful factory owner in New Lanark; see chapter four
10. See note four
11. For a discussion of these changes in the party see Cornford, J. (1963) 'The Transformation of Conservatism in the late Nineteenth Century', *Victorian Studies* vol. VII no. 3
12. See Feuchtwanger, E. J. (1959) 'The Conservative Party under the impact of the Second Reform Act', *Victorian Studies* vol. II no. 4
13. *The Radical Programme* (1885). Chapman and Hall: London, quoted in Garvin, J. L. (1933) *The Life of Joseph Chamberlain* volume II, Macmillan: London, p. 57. *The Radical Programme* has been reprinted with an introduction by Hamer, D. A. (1971) Harvester Press: Brighton
14. Factory Acts Extension Bill 1867
15. Hours of Labour Regulation Bill 1867
16. P. Smith (1967) *Disraelian Conservatism and Social Reform.* Routledge and Kegan Paul: London; University of Toronto Press: Toronto
17. Working Class Dwellings Act 1885, Housing of the Working Classes Act 1890, Public Health Act 1890
18. Factory and Workshop Act 1890
19. Shop Hours Act 1892
20. Technical Instruction Act 1889; Intermediate Education Act 1889

Chapter four
SOCIALISM

POLITICAL THEORY

The political theory of nineteenth-century British Socialism exhibits a wide range of attitudes towards and beliefs about industrial society professed by a bewildering variety of individuals and organisations. At one end of the spectrum of ideas we find socialism rejecting the values of industrial capitalism – materialism, competition, the pursuit of economic growth – and its institutions. This kind of socialism offers an alternative society based on the values of co-operation, brotherhood, and the pursuit of communal interests, a simple life which turns men away from the pursuit of material wealth. At the other end of the spectrum we find the acceptance of industrialism and its benefits but a rejection of its forms of organisation and the distribution of its material benefits. Socialism is here presented as a mechanism by which the efficiency of production might be increased and the benefits made available to all. This distinction between rejection and reform of industrial society, though crude, is a useful device for beginning to understand socialist theory but it is not a rigid classification. The ideas expressed by different 'schools' of socialist thought in the nineteenth century and by individual socialist thinkers often contain a mixture of both the views outlined. Neither can the development of socialism in the nineteenth century be presented as a neat chronological progression from a total rejection of industrial society to its gradual acceptance.

This picture is further complicated by the fact that socialism was not the only school of thought which presented such critiques of society. There was a strong element in Conservatism which was based on a rejection of the values of industrial society and an element which demanded reform. Liberalism, whilst lacking a fundamental opposition to industrial society *per se*, did, in its various forms, present a far-reaching attack on established political institutions and the distribution of property and privilege. The problem then is to establish the distinctive features of socialism and we might begin this by a negative process – by exploring the limitations of certain categories such as the identification of socialism with collectivism and with working-class organisations.

Collectivism is itself a difficult term to define but if it is understood as referring to the desire to increase the powers of the State then it is a description which has a much wider application than the term socialist. Many Conservatives and Liberals as well as those describing themselves as socialists wished to see the range of state activities extended. Equally there were some socialists who doubted whether legislative activity could achieve their objectives. There was a tendency to use collectivism and socialism as interchangeable terms in the late nineteenth century, particularly by those unsympathetic to increased state intervention, but to do so is to produce a great deal of confusion.

To identify socialism with the political activity of the organised working class is also misleading, though there may be some grounds for doing so. In the nineteenth century it is the condition of the working class which provides the focus for socialist theory and practice, but working-class support for the Conservative and Liberal parties and for the values of individualism should not be underestimated. Working-class agitation for parliamentary reform or factory legislation, the activities of trade unions, forms of mutual aid and co-operation, were not necessarily inspired by socialist principles.

Clearly, if we are to assess socialist theory and its influence on public policy, such theory will have to be identified but a precise definition to cover the range of nineteenth-century British Socialism is not possible. Rather, what we can do is to identify key elements in the complex of values which constitute the socialist traditions and which appear in all varieties of socialism.[1] The wide range of socialist thought can then be rendered more intelligible by using the different weight given to certain values as a principle of classification. Perhaps the most important of these is the condemnation of inequality. In terms of nineteenth-century Britain this amounts to condemnation of inequalities of income and wealth, of working conditions, of social conditions – housing, health, education – and of political power. The reasons for taking condemnation of inequality as a central value rather than a positive commitment to equality are bound up with the difficulties of the concept of equality. Absolute equality, the demand that everyone should receive identical treatment in all respects, has rarely, if ever, been held by any serious political theorist. The principle of equality is most often formulated as a requirement that all persons should be treated equally unless there are good reasons for treating them differently. This, however, is a formal principle, one which tells us how to go about making a decision but does not give any indication of the substance or content of that decision; it does not tell us what is to count as a good reason. Socialists tended to be united in their criticism of nineteenth-century society, agreeing that the social, economic and political differences which existed were not based on good reasons for such differential treatment, but they showed much less unity when making proposals for a future society and when filling in the details of a new system of distribution.

The second element in nineteenth-century socialist thought was an ethical critique of capitalism and a tendency to see the task of socialism as the moral reconstruction of society. Thus the competitive, acquisitive values of capitalism set men against one another and led to exploitation, selfishness and untold human suffering. Socialism would bring about a moral transformation, fostering the spirit of social conscience, co-operation and brotherhood. This ethical approach is obviously related to the condemnation of inequality since the existence of inequality prevents the development of these moral ideals. The third element might best be characterised as a view of socialism as the most rational, efficient form of social and economic organisation. Thus, to explore the connections with the previous elements, the inequalities of capitalism were not only unjust but wasteful of human effort and potential. Socialism offered the opportunity to direct and control production and distribution in the most efficient and rational manner. The fourth element is perhaps the most vague but concerns the view that, through socialism, man might be set free from the unnatural way of life which industrial capitalism forced upon him and so realise his 'true nature'. It is important to stress that these elements in socialist thought are not exclusive and that all were present to some degree throughout the nineteenth century in all the forms which socialism took in Britain during this period. However, the analysis which follows is based on the contention that, for the purposes of understanding socialist theory in the nineteenth century, a distinction can be drawn between those thinkers who emphasise the ethical view and those who emphasise the rational efficiency view.

The man most often credited with beginning the modern socialist tradition in Britain is Robert Owen (1771–1858). He combined the ethical and rational approaches in a manner which has led to widely differing estimations of his contribution to the theory and practice of socialism and which has allowed succeeding generations of socialists to interpret him in many different ways. 'A good part of the English socialist tradition is in fact a series of re-interpretations of enigmatic figures from the past. For each age there is a new view of Mr Owen.'[2] Owen is a rationalist in the sense that he holds to a view of the perfectability of man through the development of reason and believes that human destiny is wholly in the hands of men. He is a moralist in that moral regeneration, the construction of a new system of values, and the creation of good character are the objectives to which reason must be applied; a view which he expressed in language reminiscent of the preacher. Though he was not a Christian, in the later part of his life (after 1817) many of his statements have the ring of the prophet announcing the imminent coming of salvation, the golden age, the millenium which consists of the widespread adoption of his proposed social arrangements.

Owen's lifetime spanned the maturing of industrialisation in Britain and in his career he progressed from apprentice in a draper's shop to owner, in 1800, of the largest spinning mills in Scotland, at New Lanark. He was particularly well placed to appreciate the problems and the benefits of industrial production and to have the opportunity to put into practice many of his ideas concerning social and industrial organisation. He achieved fame as a 'model employer', providing excellent working and living conditions for his labour force and educational facilities for their children, while running a highly profitable business. The theory on whch he based his achievements at New Lanark and which he developed to apply to the reform of society as a whole first appeared in four essays on the formation of human character entitled *A New View of Society* and published for sale in 1816. The evils of society – poverty, crime, human misery and conflict – are attributed by Owen to an error of judgement concerning the nature of man – the view that individuals are responsible for the formation of their own character. The truth, according to Owen, is that man's character is made for him by the circumstances, the environment in which he lives. Once this truth replaces ignorance and error 'experience will soon teach us how to form character, individually and generally, so as to give the greatest sum of happiness to the individual, and to mankind'.[3] What experience will show is that through a system of education based on this principle, and an environment in which the spirit of community, cooperation and fellowship can flourish, all men will achieve the goodness and excellence of which they are capable. In the case of children the remedial action presented no problem, for 'children are, without exception, passive and wonderfully contrived compounds (which) may be formed collectively to have any human character'.[4] Through a national system of education with properly trained teachers, children may be taught to promote the good of all. The problem of adults, whose character has already been formed by an unhealthy society, has to be tackled by reconstruction of that society. The first step would be reform of the legal system in order to discourage vice, the second to undermine those religious beliefs which stress the individual's responsibility for his own character, and the third to attack unemployment rationally and systematically. Taken together these steps would create an environment in which human nature could be transformed.

There is little in Owen's *New View of Society* which could be described as 'socialistic' apart from the implication of the right to work. The whole tone of the essays is one of benevolent paternalism, a plea directed towards men of influence and position, the truth of which, Owen believes, they will find irresistible. He also shows faith in existing political institutions and political leaders, and a rejection of parliamentary reform as a means of social transformation. This latter view he maintained consistently even when his proposals for social regeneration developed along more recognisably socialist lines. He saw the working class as ignorant and debased, through no fault of their own, and to extend the franchise to them, before the transformation of character had taken place, would be to invite anarchy and chaos. Once the transformation had been achieved then political reform would cease to be of importance as the causes of conflict would disappear. The only means of dealing with evil was the removal of ignorance and once this was achieved the particular form of government would cease to have any importance. The development of a critique of capitalism, based on condemnation of the competitive, individualist ethic and the institution of private property, came after Owen failed to elicit any response to his proposals for dealing with the rise in unemployment which occurred in 1816. Owen's analysis was based on the view that unemployment was caused by overproduction which was itself the result of the increase in machine power and the displacement of manual labour. While production increased, consumption decreased as the wages of the labouring classes declined. The problem of unemployment had to be met by balancing consumption and production. Owen proposed that Villages of Co-operation should be established in which the unemployed would be able to work to maintain themselves and their families, and educate their children. These co-operative villages were, in effect, self-sufficient communes which would have the economic benefit of dealing with unemployment and would also achieve the moral improvement of the unemployed. His proposals gained little support, a fact which Owen attributed to the false views of political economists like Ricardo and James Mill and to religion. Owen came to see that the eradication of false beliefs could only be achieved by the transformation of the system of production and distribution in which such beliefs were firmly embedded. The co-operative villages, which were first proposed as a solution to the problem of unemployment, now became the means of effecting moral regeneration and social reconstruction. This view was most clearly expressed in his *Report to the County of Lanark* (1820), a response to a request by the county authority for advice on how to remedy unemployment. The idea that man makes his own character leads to competition and the attempt to accumulate personal wealth. Production is therefore increased as a means of making greater and greater profits, but achieves only an increase in human misery and uncertainty. Owen believed that the benefits of industrial production could be so organised as to produce sufficient wealth for everyone. What was required was an environment which would produce the necessary change in character to a spirit of co-operation. This environment could only be created in small communities, where property was communally owned and where productive forces were directed to increasing the happiness of all. The problem of distribution was to be solved by the abolition of money and its replacement by labour notes. Owen argued that human labour is the 'natural' standard of value of any commodity – its worth is the amount of effort required to produce it – and that it is possible to calculate an average unit of labour power on which the exchange value of any article can be based. Whoever produced an article would receive a 'labour note' for the number of units used in its production which could be exchanged for goods of similar labour value. The power of consumption would thus match the amount of production and the distribution of goods would be fair.

It is important to note that Owen's views contained no element of class war or class conflict and that he believed in a gradual process of reform which would come about with the full consent of all once the truth was revealed. He believed that his system presented no threat to established wealth and privilege, on the grounds that the benefits which the wealthy enjoyed would be revealed as paltry compared to the advantages of life in one of his communities. The harnessing of productive power to a system based on co-operation and goodwill would produce enough for everyone and eliminate conflict. Unlike many critics of industrial society he is not opposed to industrialisation as such, nor does he seek a return to a simpler pre-industrial form of community. It is rather that industrial processes have the capacity for great evil and great benefit but the benefits can only be reaped by appreciation of the 'true' nature of character formation. The pursuit of self-interest is not a natural characteristic of human beings but a product of the environment of competitive capitalism and is therefore capable of transformation.

Owen was not the sole contributor to socialist theory in the early nineteenth century, though his enormous energy in spreading his ideas made him of undoubted importance in the development of British socialism. The 1820s also witnessed the development of anti-capitalist economic theory by individuals who were in closer contact with working-class organisations than was Owen. The central concept in this economic critique was the labour theory of value which has a long intellectual history in British radicalism. In the early nineteenth century it was the attempt of David Ricardo (1772–1823) to develop an understanding of the revolutionary developments of the industrial economy which exercised most influence on socialist thinkers. Ricardo believed that capital was the driving force of all social progress and that there was a fundamental opposition of interest between capitalists and the aristocracy, whose income derived from rent on landed property. Labour, as he understood it, was merely the instrument of capital and as such there was no opposition of interest between these two factors. Ricardo held that the natural value or price of any commodity is measured by the amount of labour necessary to produce that commodity under the most unfavourable conditions of production, and includes production costs and profit. Wages, which form part of these costs, are determined by the amount of money necessary to sustain the workman – for food, shelter, clothing – and to provide for a standard of living which varies with the customs and degree of civilisation of the area in which he lives. The activities of capital make possible this steady income which leads to an increase in the population. As population rises the demand for food rises and more and more land is turned over to agriculture, but this will be the less fertile or marginal land on which more labour will be required to produce less. The consequences will be a rise in agricultural prices to cover costs, with a corresponding increase in the surplus profit from the more fertile land which will be appropriated by the landowners in the form of rent. At the same time wages in manufacturing will rise in order to provide the necessities of life and these will cut the amount of profit. The introduction of machinery will reduce labour costs but will depress the value of goods produced since less labour, from which all value is derived, will be involved in their production. The landowning class thus grows richer without any increase in effort while the capitalist and the labourer grow poorer. The factors which produced this situation were the monopoly on the land and tariffs, such as the Corn Laws, which prevented cheap imports of food and encouraged cultivation of marginal land. The early English socialists adapted Ricardo's theory to form an attack on both the aristocracy and the capitalist class by identifying the capitalist as non-productive and by claiming the source of all value to be physical labour. Ricardo's law of wages was also modified and taken as the view that, in the capitalist system, the workman only receives enough for subsistence with the employer extracting the surplus value. Thus capital does not contribute to the value of commodities; all value is created by physical labour. Labour does not receive the full value of the goods produced but only enough for subsistence, therfore under the capitalist system the labouring classes can only increase the wealth of the employers. This was seen as the basis of the whole economic system of capitalism and any legislative reform or political action which sought to reform rather than sweep away the economic system was doomed to failure. No matter what the form of government, while the economic system remained unchanged, the position of labour would also remain unchanged.

For men like J. F. Bray (1809–1895) the solution lay in the creation of Owenite communities as a first move towards a social system based on communal ownership. For Thomas Hodgskin (1785–1869) the exploitation of labour was a result of infringements of natural rights to property and the solution lay in reasserting the right of every individual to property ownership, creating a society of independent property owners – a decidedly non-socialist solution. Socialist ideas in the 1820s and 1830s were a combination of economic analysis of this kind together with Owenite ideas of co-operation and attacks on both capital and aristocratic monopoly of the land, heavily imbued with moral condemnation of the injustice and unfairness of a system which deprived a man of the full reward of his labour.

This ferment of socialist ideas, however, died away in the 1840s. The reasons for this are complex but one might point to the failure to create a mass movement, evidenced by the collapse of Chartism, the transformation of the co-operative movement into a respectable consumers' organisation and the failure of the trade union movements to organise among the unskilled and semi-skilled workers. This in turn may be seen as a consequence of the maturing of industrial capitalism which brought with it increased prosperity for a portion of the skilled working class, the repeal of the Corn Laws, and the amelioration of cruder forms of exploitation through factory legislation. In the period from 1848 to the late 1870s socialist ideas were maintained largely by the Christian Socialists. Marx and Engels seem to have exercised little substantial influence on intellectual opinion until the 'Socialist revival' of the 1880s.

Christian Socialism, as the name implies, was an attempt to establish a union between Christianity and social life based on the principle that all men share a common humanity through their relation to God. It is in the works of F. D. Maurice (1805–1872), J. M. Ludlow (1821–1911) and Charles Kingsley (1819–1875) that the ideas of Christian Socialism were most clearly expressed. Its origins lie in a response to the political unrest of the late 1840s, the causes of which were identified as the selfishness and competition characteristic of social life, against which the task of Christian Socialism was to reassert the spirit of Christian brotherhood. Socialism was simply the assertion of God's order in this world and thus it was the business of the Church and not the State to promote '. . . an actually living community under Christ, in which no man has a right to call anything that he has his own, but in which there is spiritual fellowship and practical co-operation'.[5] Christian Socialists saw the task as an educational one, to moralise both the working class and the middle class and to achieve class reconciliation through fair and brotherly dealing in all economic affairs:

> Let us all try to love the society in which we live and we shall soon make it easy for us to live in. Let us learn to look not for differences but for agreement, seeking to reconcile divisions and not to make them, and we shall at last understand and feel what a blessing and privilege it is to be members of the Great English Partnership.[6]

This moral regeneration would see the fruition of a long and vigorous tradition in Christianity but it would not be achieved by movements seeking purely political reforms. Chartism, according to Kingsley, sought to do God's work with the devil's tools whereas the only solution was the co-operative organisation of labour under

Christian direction. Purely political objectives would not achieve moral regeneration and Owenite plans for co-operation would fail because they were not based on Christianity. The condemnation of political reform stemmed not only from the primacy of moral regeneration but also from a distrust of the mass of the population. Both Maurice and Kingsley displayed positive sympathy with the working class while supporting the existing political system. Indeed, Kingsley believed that the aristocracy was an essential element of English society and had to live up to the high calling conferred upon it. Maurice held similar views and said of the great mass of the people:[7]

> They need to be directed, to be treated as subjects, it is true, but they need also to be sympathised with, to be treated as brethren. They want a fellowship as well as a government, they want some society in which high and low, rich and poor should be permitted as equals, as well as one in which they shall receive protection and help from those whom difference in outward advantages had made their superiors.

The Christian Socialists possessed no clear programme of action but were closely involved in securing legal recognition of the co-operative movements where some notable success was achieved. However, by then co-operation was more to be identified with the principles of self-help and thrift than with the spirit of Christian co-operation which Christian Socialists had hoped would be a result of co-operative, self-governing units of production. Though the Christian Socialist movement collapsed in 1854 it reappeared in 1877 with the formation of the Anglo-Catholic Guild of St Matthew and in 1889 with the Christian Socialist Union. The identification of socialism with Christian brotherhood was later taken up by Keir Hardie and the Independent Labour Party, though this was perhaps more a case of using religious language as part of the rhetoric of socialism than a development from theology.

The revival of socialist thought from 1880 onwards drew its inspiration from many sources, including the Owenite co-operative tradition, socialist interpretations of Ricardian economics, the romantic and backward-looking condemnation of capitalism expressed by Carlyle and Ruskin, utilitarianism, and the writings of Marx and Engels. The reasons for this revival may perhaps be sought in the changing economic circumstances occasioned by the onset of the 'Great Depression' (1873–96) which brought increased unemployment and poverty. The existence of such misery was highlighted by such pamphlets as *The Bitter Cry of Outcast London*

(1883), the journalism of W. T. Stead in the *Pall Mall Gazette* and the publication, in 1881, of Henry George's *Progress and Poverty*. It is this latter work, together with George's lectures delivered in Britain in 1882, which appears to have exercised the greatest influence in directing awareness of the problems of poverty towards socialist solutions. George identified the cause of poverty as the institution of private property in land. Poverty could be removed only by making land common property, a task which, George suggested, could be achieved not by confiscation or state purchase, but by a tax on the rent from land; a tax which would replace all other forms of taxation. The revenue from this 'single tax' would then finance vastly increased public services. This identification of social problems with the malfunctioning of the economic system, frequently expressed in religious language, and the combination of both an economic and a moral critique of capitalism, proved an inspiration to a great many of the individuals who came to socialism in the last two decades of the nineteenth century. However, the first of the socialist organisations of this period, the Democratic Federation (1881), later to become the Social Democratic Federation (SDF) (1884), was avowedly Marxist.

The leader and founder of this organisation was H. M. Hyndman (1842–1921), a Tory radical who met Marx in 1880, subsequently read *Capital* and became convinced of the inevitability of socialism. Hyndman believed that the transformation of society could be achieved by constitutional means and only after failing, in 1881, to convince Disraeli that the Conservative party was the vehicle to bring about peaceful change did he turn to independent political action by founding the Federation. He produced a book, *England for All* (1881), in which he set out his ideas, appealing for the unity of the working class and insisting that if reforms were to be peaceful then the rich and powerful must lead the way. He proposed a combination of land reform, political reforms such as adult suffrage, annual parliaments and payment of members, together with increased state regulation of economic and social life. Though he had drawn heavily on Marx for his economic analysis he failed to acknowledge Marx by name, a failure which led to a breach in his relationship with Marx. In subsequent writings he rectified this, indeed he saw his task as being to 'do my utmost to spread a knowledge of his works and theories in the English speaking world: while endeavouring at the same time to ally his bolder conceptions to a more immediate policy of my own'.[8]

That immediate policy consisted of a series of practical reforms including nationalisation of the land, railways and banks; an eight-hour day; free compulsory education; free school meals and better housing, all of which would provide a series of 'stepping stones' towards Socialism. In spite of his rhetoric, which was often militant and revolutionary, Hyndman accepted the role of the State in transforming society and saw the task of socialists as 'teaching mankind the truth about the relentless but unconscious or unappreciated development towards Collectivism and Socialism'.[9] In particular this consisted of giving to the working class a thorough understanding of their exploited condition and of the need for political action guided by socialist principles. The cornerstone of Hyndman's theory was a dogmatic belief in the inevitable collapse of capitalism brought about by its internal contradictions. He adapted Marx's theory of surplus value to a belief in the 'iron law of wages', the view that under capitalism the 'wages on the average in every trade (will) be no more than the subsistence rate customary in that trade regulated by competition'.[10] Thus the labourer received wages only at subsistence level while the surplus value, created by his hours of work over and above those necessary to create his subsistence, was appropriated by the capitalist. The increasing immiseration of the working class as a result of built-in exploitation would lead inevitably to class conflict, economic crises and the collapse of capitalism. Therefore, no lasting improvement in social life could be achieved until the wages system was abolished and the means of production and exchange taken into public ownership. One of the major consequences of this view was Hyndman's hostility to trade unions and his denial that they could ever function as the means of raising the consciousness of the working class or play a part in the transformation to socialism. Hyndman regarded the unions as an obstruction to working-class solidarity because they represented only a minority of the 'better off' section of the working class and acted as the allies of the Liberal party. Their fight for higher wages and shorter hours fatally distracted attention away from the fact that it was the wage system itself which should be fought. Unlike Marx and Engels, Hyndman could not accept that trade union activity could lead to political awareness. This could be achieved only by socialist propaganda and organisation of the working class to pursue socialist objectives. Hyndman was quite prepared to co-operate with other socialist organisations but not with the trade unions. Though legal limitation of the working day to eight hours was one of his short-term objectives, this had to be taken along with his other 'stepping stones', not as an end in itself but as part of a transition to

socialism. Hyndman's socialism was based on an extremely mechan-
istic view of social change and though not devoid of moral condemnation of capitalism, the emphasis was on a rational, economic
approach from which he rarely deviated.

It would be misleading to present Hyndman's views as those of
the SDF as a whole since there existed notable differences of opinion
among its members. Considerable opposition existed to what was
seen as the political opportunism of Hyndman and the compromise
involved in electioneering. It was this opposition which led, in 1884,
to a split between William Morris and Hyndman and the formation
of the Socialist League under the leadership of Morris.

William Morris (1834–1896) became a socialist late in life, joining
the Democratic Federation in 1883, and subsequently became one
of the most active contributors, through his lectures and writings,
to 'the cause' of socialism. By this time Morris had already established an enormous reputation as a poet, a scholar of medieval and
Norse history, an artist and designer. Intellectually he had been
much influenced by the writings of Carlyle and Ruskin and shared
their views on the evils of modern civilisation: the reduction of
human relationships to cash payments, the removal of the dignity
of labour and creative work by machinery and the division of labour,
and the ugliness of all the products of industrial society. Though
Morris's early work may bear the stamp of a longing for the
simplicity and purity of medieval life, and a romanticised view of
feudal society, by the late 1870s he had come to see the need for a
fundamental remedy to the ills of contemporary society. It was
through reading J. S. Mill that Morris realised that socialism was
a necessary change but it was Marx's *Capital* and conversations with
men like Hyndman which led him to an understanding of the nature
of that change and a commitment to 'practical socialism' as the
culmination of his previous ideas.

Morris's socialism centres around the relationship between Art
and Labour but 'Art' here is understood as the product of the
creative capabilities which all human beings possess. It is through
labour that such capabilities, which are fundamental to human life,
receive their expression: 'Art is man's embodied expression of
interest in the life of man; it springs from man's pleasure in his life'
and his 'daily necessary work which expresses itself and is embodied
in that work itself'.[11] The capitalist system of production with its
search for profit, division of labour and machine production had
destroyed this expression of man's humanity, as evidenced by the
ugliness and shoddiness of its products and the poverty and degra-

dation of the mass of the people. Machinery, far from minimising painful labour and freeing men for creative work, had replaced creative work. Morris found in Marx the historical understanding of the development of capitalism and the dynamics of change: 'Commercialism, competition has sown the wind recklessly and must reap the whirlwind; it has created the proletariat for its own interest, and its creation will and must destroy it: there is no other force which can do so.'[12]

Only socialism could provide the conditions for fruitful labour. Common ownership of the means of production and equality of condition were not merely desirable but necessary to a properly ordered society where everyone willing to work would be ensured honourable and fitting work, a healthy and beautiful house, and full leisure for rest of mind and body. Such a change could not come about through the reforming actions of the middle classes because they were slaves to the commercial system. All reforms were dismissed as 'palliatives' and those supporting them condemned for foolish optimism. Though Owen and the Chartists were praised for keeping alive the discontent of the working class, Morris claimed that Owen had failed to see that the privileged class in executive power would never allow any tampering with the system which maintained them, while the Chartists had thought it possible to have political freedom with economic slavery.

Socialism could only be achieved by revolution: 'The basis of all change must be as it always has been, the antagonism of the classes.'[13] What then was to be the nature of this revolution and how might it be brought about? Morris saw his task as 'stirring up discontent' and 'making socialists', spreading socialist ideas among the working class in order to develop a revolutionary consciousness. He was, for many years, fiercely critical of all political action, which he saw as both ineffective and, more importantly, as leading to the corruption of socialist ideals. He was also suspicious of trade unions which he felt had become conservative and obstructive bodies wielded by middle-class politicians for party purposes. It was not until the last two years or so of his life that he modified these views and accepted the validity of using the extended franchise as a means of achieving socialism. Even then he was insistent that any such political activity should be achieved by a genuinely socialist party and that the aim should be not merely improvement but a fundamental change in the position of the working class. Morris was not optimistic about the attainment of such a transformation through political means as can be seen in *News from Nowhere*, his vision of the future society which was to come into being in the year 1952. In a chapter entitled 'How the Change Came', it is as a result of partial state socialism unbalancing the commercial system that the confusion, suffering and discontent which leads to violence and revolution is brought about. The time scale should convey Morris's increasing doubts about the immediacy of social transformation, while the future society which *News from Nowhere* depicts is a clear illustration of the ethical, aesthetic and libertarian cast of his socialism.

The intellectual climate of the early 1880s provided many different forms of expression for those individuals concerned about social conditions and individual and social morality. The proliferation of organisations, debating societies, discussion groups, both formal and informal, allowed for a considerable interchange of ideas and personnel which goes some way towards explaining the breadth of socialism in this period. The early years of the Fabian Society are perhaps the clearest illustration of the process by which such a broad spread of ideas was gradually shaped into a more precise social philosophy. The origins of the Fabian Society lie in a group formed in 1882 to discuss the ideas of Thomas Davidson. Davidson, described as a wandering teacher, saw the development of the highest moral character in individuals as the means of transforming social life. He hoped to bring together individuals capable and desirous of developing a rational morality directed towards self-perfection. From such small groups, organised into communities following the principles of 'insight, love and well-directed labour',[14] the spiritual and thus the social life of society as a whole would begin to be changed. By the end of 1883 a division of interest in the original group led to a split. Those who supported individual moral regeneration as the key to social reform formed 'The Fellowship of the New Life' while a group led by Hubert Bland and Frank Podmore, which believed that social reform must precede moral improvement, formed the Fabian Society. The name of the Society was derived from the tactics of the Roman General Fabius Cunctator who, in his battle against Hannibal, had delayed his strike until the most opportune moment. The purpose of the Fabian Society was to delay action until careful study revealed the direction which it was to take. The first year of the Society's existence was spent in considering a wide variety of approaches to the question of social reform and discussions were held on Henry George, Marx, Anarchism, Utopian Socialism and the SDF. Not until 1884 did the society formally commit itself to Socialism and even then its interpretation was wide enough to gain the support of Marxists and anarchists as well as Liberals, progressive radicals and Christian Socialists. The emergence of a more specific Fabian Socialism was largely due to the influence of George Bernard Shaw (1856–1951) and Sydney Webb (1859–1947) and has its clearest expression in the *Fabian Essays* published in 1889.

Shaw and Webb had been members of the 'Hampstead Marx Circle' formed in 1885 to discuss the works of Marx. The group rejected Marx's economic analysis along with the class struggle as the driving force of history. Marx's theory of surplus value and the labour theory of value on which it was based were also considered inadequate. Fabian economic analysis was based instead on an expanded concept of rent. Whereas Ricardo insisted on labour as the sole source of value and applied the concept of rent only to land, the Fabians extended this to include capital and skill – just as differences in the fertility of land resulted in equal labour producing different values, so differences in capital and in ability or skill led to equal labour producing different values. All surplus was therefore a form of rent, a product of 'monopolies' of land, capital and skill, which were either the result of accidents of nature or were socially formed, as for example, through education. This concept of rent undermined a whole series of assumptions on which private property was based, most notably 'the a priorist notion that among free competitors wealth must go to the industrious, and poverty be the just and natural punishment of the lazy and improvident'.[15] It also altered the interpretation of the exploitation of capitalist society. It was not, as Marx suggested, the exploitation of one class by another – indeed, the 'exploiting class' included everyone with an income above subsistence level – but exploitation of society as a whole. Rent is a product of social forces and general development and, therefore, should be appropriated for the community as a whole through progressive taxation, nationalisation and municipal ownership. The abolition of the wage system, or any similar action, will not get rid of economic rent which will always exist owing 'to the bounty of Nature or the advantage of situation'.[16] Socialisation of rent through common ownership is therefore the only course of action but it must be a gradual process with compensation for property, a method which will 'satisfy the moral sense of the ordinary citizen as effectively as that of the skilled economist'.[17]

The concept of 'final utility' is also crucial to the argument for ownership and regulation of economic life. The final utility theory of value, derived from the work of the economists Jevons and

Marshall, states that the exchange value of a commodity is fixed by the utility of the least useful part of the stock which, in turn, is determined by the supply of such a commodity. To use an illustration from Shaw, 'One umbrella is very useful: a second umbrella is a luxury: a third is mere lumber.'[18] Since an increase in supply will devalue even the most useful commodity, capitalism is characterised by gigantic conspiracies to control supply. However, the man whose only commodity for sale is his labour has practically no control over the supply of that commodity. Increasing population forces down the value of labour and leads to increased poverty and misery for the majority while the riches of a minority increase. The purchasing power of this minority 'represents no longer utility, but the cravings of lust, folly, vanity, gluttony and madness, technically defined by genteel economists as "effective demand" '.[19] Socialism demonstrated the artificial nature of the system and the need for change through an attack on the institution of private property and the development of a well-regulated economy.

Fabian Socialism was characterised not only by this economic theory but also by an interpretation of history which distinguished it from earlier socialist thought as well as from Marxism. Webb, particularly, sought a theory of socialism which would take account of the economic, social and political changes of nineteenth-century Britain. The result was a combination of many intellectual approaches – the positivism of Comte, the evolutionary theories of Spencer and Darwin and the centrality of economic factors to social change taken from Marx – which produced an evolutionary and dynamic view of socialism. The future society which socialism aimed at should not be seen as static but as an organism which would be in a constant state of change and development. This was the basis of Webb's criticisms of the 'Utopias' envisaged by men like Owen: that 'they took no account of the blind social forces which they could not control, and which went on inexorably working out salvation in ways unsuspected by the Utopian'.[20] It is history, allied to an understanding of evolutionary processes, which affords understanding of the present and gives the clue to future development. Thus individualism is seen by Webb not as a fundamental truth about human nature but as the product of a particular stage of economic and social development; an inevitable result of the economic blundering of governments in the eighteenth century which he attributes to government interference uninformed by a scientific understanding of economic law. Webb identifies three periods, or stages, in the social development of the nineteenth century. First, 'The Disintegration of the Old Synthesis', a period in which the development of industrialisation broke down the political system based on agriculture and set in motion the progress towards democracy. This was followed by a 'Period of Anarchy', a period in which there followed the individualist reaction to the political, economic and social controls of the past. However, this period also produced its own reaction, manifested not only in the works of Carlyle and Ruskin and the concept of the social organism developed by Comte, Spencer and Mill but in the practical necessity of government regulation. Such are the forces which lead to the third stage, 'The New Synthesis', and the recognition of the organic, interdependent nature of society. Thus, Webb believed that history itself was leading towards social regeneration and that it is a natural law of social organisms that they move towards increasing social unity. However powerful such a process might be it can either be promoted or resisted by the actions of individuals.

The task of the Fabian was to develop the rational, scientific understanding of the underlying tendencies and to promote those arrangements which would benefit the community as a whole. Most significant among these tendencies was the progress towards democracy, the awareness of which led to what Webb was later to call 'the inevitability of gradualness'; the transition to socialism must come through democratic, peaceful and constitutional change.[21] It was this belief in the power of rational argument, based on thorough investigation of the facts, together with the faith in constitutional procedures at both national and local level, which led to the strategy of 'permeation'. 'Permeation' meant converting significant individuals and organisations to the principles of socialism and putting into effect parts of the Fabian programme no matter what the political affiliations of such individuals and organisations might be. The important thing was that the movement towards socialism should be based on Fabian instruction. Accordingly the Society produced a mass of literature on the widest possible range of topics, containing detailed statistics and proposals for action. Fabians contested local elections for boards of guardians, school boards and town councils and maintained contact with radical clubs, members of the Liberal and Conservative parties, and senior civil servants as well as the trade unions and socialist organisations. The Fabians saw this spreading of socialist ideas as an essential first step towards creating the conditions under which a separate Socialist party might successfully be established but it was one which laid them open to charges of a high degree of equivocation on the need for a separate party and a failure to appreciate the role of the working class in bringing about socialism. This view was reinforced, to a large extent, by the primacy accorded by the Fabians to the London-based nucleus of the Society: 'We did not urge the formation of branches on luke-warm adherents and we always recognised that the peculiar methods of the London Society, appropriate to a body of highly educated people, nearly all of them speakers, writers or active political work-ers, were unsuitable for the groups of earnest workmen in the pro-vinces who were influenced by our teaching'.[22]

There was also criticism of illiberal tendencies in Fabian theory, particularly in the subordination of the individual to the improve-ment of the social organism which is implied by the need to realise that 'the perfect and fitting development of each individual is not necessarily the utmost and highest activation of his own personality, but the filling, in the best possible way, of his humble function in the great social machine'.[23] This concern for national efficiency and its connection with imperialism alienated many New Liberal theo-rists in the first decade of the twentieth century as well as placing the Fabians outside the mainstream of British socialist attitudes towards the empire. To this may be added the suspicion that 'the creation of a highly centralised machine, so delicately specialised in structure and as intricate and secret in its workings as to be incapable of any real control on the part of the electorate appears to be the conscious programme of Mr Webb and his associates'.[24] Certainly the role of the 'expert' looms large in Fabian theory and it has been pointed out that the whole of their socialism pivots on the import-ance of the professional administrator and adviser, a new and growing class in the nineteenth century and one to which the most influential Fabians themselves belonged. It is a suspicion which is not without some justification, given Webb's frequently expressed reservations about the importance of elections and the capacities of the mass of the population to understand the principles of socialism. Neither was Webb alone in seeing popular politics as an arena for manufacturing consent rather than a mechanism for registering demands: 'We did what all active politicians in a democratic country must do; we decided what the people ought to want and endea-voured to do two things which, after all are much the same thing, to make the people want it and to make it appear that they wanted it.'[25] The main objective of the Fabians, however, remained the generation of 'light without heat', the careful and thorough inves-tigation of the facts and the playing down of ethical and emotional arguments for socialism. As such, it was never intended, nor was it ever likely, to be a vehicle for creating mass support for socialism. This achievement is most usually credited to the Independent Labour Party and, more particularly, to its chief propagandist, Robert Blatchford (1851–1943) and its leading politician, Keir Hardie (1856–1914).

The Independent Labour Party (ILP) was founded in 1893 with the objectives of achieving collective ownership of the means of production, distribution and exchange and securing representation in parliament through a separate Labour party. This latter objective involved winning the support of a large section of the working class and the trade unions – a task which was not always compatible with strict adherence to socialist principles and forced a concentration on 'labourist' rather than 'socialist' issues. What this meant was a tendency to focus on the promotion of the short-term interests of labour within the capitalist system, for example legal rights of trade unions, limitation of the working day, abolition of overtime and piecework, rather than the transformation of the capitalist system itself. The compromise which such a course of action entailed produced splits in the party and although disputes over strategy can never be fully separated from questions of theory it is possible to identify a brand of socialism which is characteristic of the early ILP.

ILP socialism is one to which the epithet 'ethical' can most clearly be applied. For Hardie, 'Socialism, like every other problem of life, is at bottom a question of ethics or morals,'[26] a question in answer to which socialism offered a vision of spiritual fulfilment in a society based on co-operation and brotherhood. It was an aspiration which was frequently expressed in religious terms. Socialism thus became a 'glorious Gospel' and

> the socialist who denounces rent and interest as robbery, and who seeks the abolition of the system which legalises such, is in the true line of apostolic succession with the pre-Christian era prophets, with the Divine Founder of Christianity and with those who, for the first seven hundred years of the Christian faith, maintained even to the death the unsullied right of their religious faith to be regarded as the Gospel of the poor.[27]

Although Robert Blatchford, editor of the *Clarion* newspaper and author of *Merrie England*, was less inclined to such religious imagery he also saw socialism as the means to achieve perfection in human life: 'My ideal is frugality of body and opulence of mind,'[28] a vision of perfection which expressed in secular terms the tenets of nonconformist religious belief. *Merrie England*, which was originally written as a series of articles for the *Clarion*, achieved sales of over two million copies when published in book form. Blatchford's intention was to recruit support for socialism, and *Merrie England* is accordingly directed more to the benefits of life under socialism than to the details of its organisation and establishment. Capitalism is attacked for its waste, its ugliness, its effects on the health of the population and its belief in gain as the driving force of society, all of which Blatchford claimed was not mere rhetoric but based on fact which the reader could test by observation. Socialism was the only remedy and was to be achieved by common ownership through state monopoly which could provide the opportunity for a healthy and natural life, a country self-sufficient in food, an unpolluted environment, the rebuilding of towns, recreation, parks and libraries. Such exaggerated claims may have proved both a boon and a curse to the active politicians like Hardie but his version of socialism, though more muted and internationalist, did not differ fundamentally from that of Blatchford. One could, of course, claim with justification that there was no theoretical divide because there was no theory, merely a series of attitudes and assumptions wide enough to generate consent among all men of conscience who felt some dissatisfaction with existing conditions. Thus socialism was identified with a vague idea of a better life towards which society was already moving inevitably and gradually. Here there was no reference to class struggle or revolution, to conflict or tension, but an optimism about the possibility of using the existing machinery of the State to bring about socialism. It is hardly surprising that ILP supporters could see the road to socialism as one down which one could cycle as a member of a Clarion cycling club or along which one could take to hills and moors for weekend hikes. However, although it is easy to deride such views of socialism it is also easy to underestimate their importance within the Labour movement. The eclectic nature of ILP socialism, drawing on religious belief, the co-operative movement, Fabianism and William Morris and perhaps, above all, the respectability of its ideas, provided the framework through which mass support for the Labour party could be generated.

PRACTICAL PROPOSALS

In terms of the theory of socialism in nineteenth-century Britain it is almost impossible to point to a unity of ideas or a clearly identifiable theoretical base out of which the varieties of socialism grew. What made a socialist a socialist is much more to be found in the mode of thinking about the social, political and economic system; a sharing of attitudes or what were earlier identified as tendencies and specifically the tendency to see the ills of society in terms of the overall structure of capitalism.

It is to the practical proposals put forward for dealing with those ills that we must now turn and these will be considered under the headings of parliamentary reform, the land question, trade unions and social reform, since these issues were in the forefront of political debate throughout the century.

The movement for parliamentary reform in the period before 1832 included not only members of the middle class, seeking to take their place in a political system dominated by the landed aristocracy, but also members of the urban working class who shared in the attack on aristocratic privilege. The picture is not, however, a simple one of the new forces created by industrialisation uniting against the forces of the old order since, in some areas of the industrial north, the working class regarded the new manufacturing class as the prime enemy. The picture is further complicated by the fact that of those members of the working class supporting the movement for reform, some subscribed to the political ideas of the radicals whilst others could be described as socialists informed largely by the ideas of Owen. Working-class support therefore divided roughly between those seeking inclusion in the reformed political system and those viewing political reform as a means to changing the structure of society as a whole. The position of Owen himself on the question of parliamentary reform was, however, clear. Owen set himself the task of rescuing man from the misery of industrial life as it was then organised, and the errors on which such a life was based could only be removed by the formation of co-operative communities. Parliamentary reform would leave such errors intact and was therefore a worthless cause deflecting the attention of men from the fundamental problems of the existing system. Some of the leaders of the politically organised working class, though subscribing to Owenite criticisms of capitalism and supporting co-operation, viewed the situation differently, seeing parliamentary reform and access to political power as essential to effecting far-reaching change.

The issue of parliamentary reform could both unite men of differing political views and divide those with a common political perspective. This is perhaps best illustrated by the most formidable of the organisations seeking reform in the early part of the century – the Chartist movement. Chartism was a focus for many discontents – a reaction to the limited changes brought about by the 1832

Reform Act, the threats presented by the 1834 Poor Law Amendment Act, and the increasing use of machinery in industrial production – and was supported by socialists and non-socialists alike. There is nothing in the Charter itself which can be identified as socialist. The People's Charter originated in the London Working Men's Association and was published in 1838 demanding the vote for every male over twenty-one years of age, equal electoral districts, abolition of the property qualification for parliamentary candidates, annual parliaments, the secret ballot and payment of members. As national support for the Charter spread, so the centre of Chartism moved away from London into the provinces, incorporating more and more diverse elements. The divisions which this produced in the Chartist movement were by no means clear-cut. Just as the radical/socialist division did not represent a clear polarity of attitude, neither did the division between 'physical force' and 'moral force' as a means to achieving the immediate aims of the Charter. This latter division was between those who held that the Charter would only be achieved by creating fear in the governing class and that everything should be done to make the movement as threatening as possible, and those who believed that success could come only through educating the working man and gaining the support of men from all classes for their demands. These were the extremes but there were many who held intermediate positions where the division became much more blurred. Socialists in the Chartist movement could be found across the whole physical/moral force spectrum and if to this is added the regional variation in economic conditions and experience, it soon becomes obvious that any generalisation about Chartism is subject to intense qualification. However, as far as socialist thought within the movement is concerned, it appears that in the period up to 1848 the Owenite co-operative view was in the ascendance but that after that period it was the socialism of Ernest Jones and George Julian Harney which came increasingly to the fore and indeed transformed what remained of the Chartist movement into something approaching an openly socialist party after 1850. Theirs was an internationalist approach, much influenced by Marx and Engels, which saw the battle for enfranchisement as part of the struggle of the working class against monopoly capitalism. By this time, however, the main force of Chartism was spent and the demand for parliamentary reform passed largely into the hands of the radicals.

As we have seen, during the middle years of the century socialism became moribund and the Christian Socialists were by no means democrats. By the time of the socialist revival in the last two decades of the century the Reform Acts of 1867 and 1884 had been passed and democracy had become a partly achieved situation rather than a distant ideal. There were still those, like William Morris, who opposed parliamentary action but among socialists in this period there was almost unanimous support for universal adult suffrage, payment of members, abolition of the House of Lords and annual or triennial parliaments. If, as the Fabians suggested, the problem was not so much how to secure more political power for the people as how to persuade them to make sensible use of the power they had, then it is understandable that the major debate among socialists concerned political strategy and specifically whether or not there was a need for a separate, independent party and what the nature of that party should be. It was an issue which not only divided the socialist organisations one from another but also produced internal divisions in these organisations. In the SDF the question of political action led to the breakaway of the Socialist League but the difficulties were not thereby resolved. The crux of the problem of strategy for the SDF lay in its belief in both the efficacy of reform through parliamentary action and the possibility of a sudden transformation of society. In practice the SDF found itself preaching the need for a political organisation based on a pure socialist ideology and yet, at the same time, pursuing 'opportunist' electoral deals with its ideological and political opponents. Most notable among these was the 'Tory Gold' incident at the general election of 1885 during the campaign for which the SDF accepted financial help from a Conservative agent, Maltman Barry. The crucial question for the SDF, however, was its relationship to other socialist organisations and the extent to which it should support a move towards 'Socialist Unity', particularly after the 1895 election in which all socialist candidates had failed so badly. In this period the SDF appear to have been willing to move towards unification with the Independent Labour Party and, in 1897, it was the ILP members and not the SDF who blocked this development. It was the implacable opposition of the SDF to the trade unions, on the grounds that they were not socialist organisations, and fear of the electoral consequences of Hyndman's Marxism which led to ILP withdrawal. The SDF was prepared to support a new single party but only one which included other socialist organisations and it was indeed represented on the Labour Representative Committee set up in 1900 which was to lead to the formation of the Labour party. By 1901 the SDF had withdrawn and again the issue of affiliation with the trade unions was the crucial element. The SDF accepted the need for friendly relations with trade unions and expressed sympathy for their struggle for better conditions but could not accept 'an alliance with the trade unions which might bind us to support men and measures with which the SDF cannot agree'.[29] Thereafter the gulf widened and the SDF determined to remain outside the Labour party until it committed itself to socialism. In 1909 the SDF changed its name to the Social Democratic Party and formed the basis of the British Socialist Party set up in 1911, which itself led to the formation of the Communist Party of Great Britain in 1920. The issues which brought about this separation remain unresolved.

The Fabian Society was also involved in internal dispute and argument with other socialist organisations when confronted with the issue of independent political action. In theory the Fabian position on democracy was plain. Based on an optimistic view of the results of an extension of the franchise, the Fabians believed that through representative democracy the machinery of the state could be used to bring about a socialist society. Democracy provided the means by which the machinery of government could be directed towards socialism and by which popular control might be exercised over the 'experts' so necessary to Fabian ideas of policy-making. However, on the question of whether or not an independent socialist party was a necessary part of such a progress there existed a divergence of views. The Fabian Tract (Number 49 1894) *A Plan of Campaign for Labour* looked to a separate party based on socialist principles and having extensive trade union support. Such a party, however, could only be effective when a programme of education had created the necessary understanding of and support for socialist principles among the electors. The major strategy of the Fabians, however, was one of permeation of radical organisations with socialist proposals and ideas, and particularly the hope that the Liberal party might be directed towards socialism. It was a strategy which was pursued most vigorously in the London County Council. There is no necessary contradiction between the two strategies outlined above; certainly it is possible to see permeation as a preliminary to the emergence of an independent party or to see an independent party as a necessary step should permeation fail. In practice, however, the two views proved difficult to reconcile within the Fabian Society and as a result it proved difficult to remove the scepticism which the other socialist organisations, particularly the ILP, felt about Fabian attitudes to independent political action. Although the Fabians supported the creation of the ILP in 1893, they did not support the move towards a united Socialist party which began in

1894, largely because of the presence of the SDF. By the time of the creation of the Labour Representation Committee in 1900, Fabian enthusiasm for a trade union-based Socialist party also seems to have waned: 'They had grown more cynical since those days: their attention was turned elsewhere; they were "permeating" in high official and political circles; but not least it also appeared to them that the LRC of 1900 was obtaining trade union support at the price of its Socialism.'[30] When the Labour party was finally established in 1906 it was not a Socialist party, but this did not mean a retreat into sectarianism for the Fabians as it did for the SDF. The Fabians continued to be active both inside and outside the Labour party in promoting their socialist ideas and proposals for reform.

The Independent Labour Party, as its title implies, faced no such dilemmas as the Fabians on permeation and independence. The ILP line was quite clear that there was a need for a new party, independent of Conservatives and Liberals, which could only succeed with the active co-operation of the trade unions. However, there remained a constant problem of the extent to which trade union support could be achieved without sacrificing socialist principles. The breakdown of the proposed alliance with the SDF seems to indicate the awareness which ILP leaders had of the need to proceed with extreme caution in view of much trade union hostility towards socialism. By the late 1890s the ILP had come to accept the need for a broad alliance of Labour interests rather than a distinctly socialist alliance as the means by which their objectives could be achieved. It was an ILP resolution at the Trade Union Congress of 1899 which led to such an alliance and the formation of the LRC in 1900, the purpose of which was to establish a distinct Labour group in parliament. In many ways this was the beginning and not the end of the problems within the ILP. With the advent of a non-socialist Labour party in 1906 the division between the rank and file of the ILP and its leadership, particularly those in parliament, became more apparent. Impatience at the failure to promote socialist policies, frustration at the political compromise and playing down of socialism in order to gain electoral and trade union support, led to intense internal battles in the ILP in the period up to the outbreak of the First World War.

The question of the relationship between socialists and trade unions was central to the political strategy of the socialists in the late nineteenth century and it is one which requires some clarification. The trade unions were not the creation of socialists, and though the Combination Acts of 1799–1800 had made them illegal they had not prevented their existence. In the first three decades of the nineteenth century trade unions were confined to fairly small-scale craft-based local organisations for mutual aid and limited to economic objectives. Only in the early 1830s do we see the emergence of larger-scale organisations influenced by socialist ideas and pursuing wider political and economic goals. In this period, partly due to the frustration of aspirations for parliamentary reform and the influence of Owenite ideas, there developed a number of unions whose objective was to transform society by extra-parliamentary means. Of these the most celebrated is the Grand National Consolidated Trade Union, founded in 1834 and headed by Owen, which sought to unite the working class and bring about the Owenite ideal of community and co-operation. This was a short-lived phase and the national unions did not survive internal division, lack of organisation and financial weakness. Established trade unions stood back and continued their struggles for better pay and conditions, and by August 1834 the 'general' union movement had collapsed. The influence of socialists on trade unions in the succeeding decades up to 1880 was minimal. The exact nature of the trade union movement in the mid-nineteenth century is the subject of debate among historians but some generalisations outlining the parameters of that debate might usefully be made, provided that the existence of more complex questions is recognised. The debate centres on the changes in working-class politics and the exact reasons for such changes, but we might identify in broad terms a shift towards a less ambitious set of demands and aspirations, what one historian has identified as a shift from a 'knife and fork' question to a 'collar and tie' question,[31] that is, a move towards gaining respectability and acceptance – away from working-class separation and towards recognition and inclusion in the existing system. As far as the trade unions are concerned there was a shift away from the general union of the working class towards building national unions based on skills and concentrating on control over their particular jobs and conditions rather than over wider economic and social conditions. This period sees the growth and spread of 'New Model Unions' based mainly on the better-off, skilled sections of the working class, offering not only machinery for the protection and improvement of wages but Friendly Society benefits such as unemployment and sickness insurance. The trade unions were involved in the campaign for parliamentary reform prior to the 1867 Reform Act but their major political activity concerned the battle for legal recognition. In 1869 the Labour Representation League was formed to promote the election of working-class candidates, two of whom were elected in 1874 and took the Liberal Whip, cementing the relationship between the political activity of organised Labour and the Liberal party – the Lib-Lab alliance. In legislative terms the trade unions enjoyed steady if not continuous progress. The Trade Union Act 1871 brought legal recognition of the unions while the Criminal Law Amendment Act 1871 prohibited picketing. In 1875 the latter act was replaced by the Conspiracy and Protection of Property Act which once again made picketing legal, and the Employers and Workmen Act abolished imprisonment for breach of contract. Trade union acitivity did not, however, spread to any great extent among the lower paid and unskilled until the emergence in 1889 of the 'new unions'. It is at this point that socialists reappear in the arena of trade union activity. In the period 1889–91 trade union membership doubled, extending particularly to the unskilled labourers in shipyards and building, gasworkers and dockers. How far these 'new unions' embodied a movement towards a wider view of working-class solidarity and acceptance of socialist ideas is open to question but it is undoubtedly true that socialists were involved in this upsurge of union activity. Tom Mann and Will Thorne, both SDF members, led the Dockers' Union and Gasworkers and General Labourers' Union respectively, but the SDF as an organisation gave little support, reflecting the view so vigorously held by Hyndman that the campaign for socialism was of greater importance than the particular concerns of groups of workers. It is illustrative of this attitude that the SDF, which had vigorously supported the agitation of the unemployed in London in 1886 and 1887, drew back from involvement in union organisation two years later. Nevertheless, socialists had gained an important access to the trade union movement. Union activists thereafter included many who identified themselves as socialists – though Lib-Labism dominated the TUC for many years, making the task of persuading the unions of the need for an independent party extremely difficult and of committing that party to socialism even more so. The SDF, though supporting the eight-hour day and a legal minimum wage, virtually ruled itself out of these tasks through its hostility to trade unions as non-socialist bodies and it was the Fabian Society and, more importantly, the ILP, who recognised the importance of the trade unions to the achievement of socialism.

Support for the recognition of trade union rights became a central plank of the socialist platform. Fabian proposals were characteristically detailed, covering the eight-hour day, stricter implementation and extension of Factory Acts, control over 'sweated' industries, the implementation of a national minimum wage backed by compulsory state arbitration and wage boards, and more effective workmen's compensation for accidents. These proposals were not particularly original nor socialist and were subscribed to by the ILP, by the trade unions and by some members of the Liberal party. The major differences between the ILP and the Fabians on these issues seems to have concerned the extent to which they saw the demands and the initiatives of the trade union movement as being in conflict with wider objectives. There were also several important differences of opinion on particular issues, most notably after the Taff Vale judgement in 1901 made unions liable for losses incurred by an employer as a result of strike action. The ILP supported a return to a pre-Taff Vale situation while Sydney Webb, who was a member of the Royal Commission on trade disputes set up in 1903, supported the Commission's recommendation that trade unions should remain liable for the action of their members only where these had been expressly authorised by an executive committee. Webb, in fact, extended this view into a proposal that compulsory arbitration should replace the right to strike, a view which was totally opposed by the TUC and the ILP.

Though socialists towards the end of the nineteenth century supported trade union demands, not solely on the grounds of political expediency but because they saw fulfilment of such demands as essential to the realisation of socialism, it is difficult to see socialist proposals as constituting an initiative. By and large socialists were supporting long-established trade union policies and where there was a conflict of ideas the trade union view triumphed.

A survey of socialist proposals on the land question might at first seem tangential to a body of theory which takes the opposition between capital and labour as its central thesis. However, the land question remained central to both socialist and radical politics throughout the nineteenth century and the popularity of Henry George's work, based on land reform, is testimony to the importance of the issue even in the mature capitalism of the 1880s. In this later period, though the connection between the working class and the land was not so immediate or recent as in the early part of the nineteenth century, land and capital had become more difficult to separate, the defection of members of the Liberal party to the Conservative party perhaps underlining this. Land also had a very great symbolic value to socialists since, of all the forms of property, it did not owe its creation to the labour of the individual who owned it.

The theoretical arguments for common ownership of the land

have already been explored; what remains now is to look at the practical proposals for effecting that common ownership. What is noticeable is the shift away from the small-scale communities proposed by Owen, the rejection of land tenure reform and peasant proprietorship, and the widespread acceptance among socialists of the need for land nationalisation and municipal ownership. It was in the Chartist movement that these divisions of opinion on land began to open up most clearly. The Chartist Land Plan, which was the child of Feargus O'Connor, sought to settle English workmen on the land as smallholders. Although the plan enjoyed great popularity within the Chartist movement, the socialists regarded it as reactionary and individualistic and their proposals in the Chartist Programme of 1851 were largely based on the ideas of Bronterre O'Brien who put forward the view that the State alone should have the power to lease land and to make use of rents. Thus nationalisation of all land, with every citizen having the right to become a tenant farmer under the State and to receive from the State a loan for initial finance, became the basis of the socialists' programme within the Chartist movement. Land nationalisation provides a continuity in policy proposals with the platform of British socialists after the revival of socialism from 1880 onwards. In the last two decades of the century there was substantial agreement on this issue between the SDF, the Fabians and the ILP. The ILP programme of 1895 included municipal ownership of land, renting out of small allotments by the municipal authority, together with farms directly managed by the authority, and the acquisition of powers by local authorities for compulsory purchase of land. Such a programme gave the socialists a policy which clearly separated them from those who sought merely a reform of the system of land tenure and from Chamberlain's proposals to restore a system of peasant proprietorship. Land nationalisation was not, however, the sole province of socialists, supported as it was by non-socialist followers of Henry George and by progressive Liberals. What characterised the socialist policy on land was the linking of the demand for land nationalisation with nationalisation of industrial capital since there existed no possibility 'of maintaining any hard and fast lines between them, either as regards their characteristics and importance in developed societies, or the defensibility of their private ownership or the arguments for their nationalisation'.[32] Thus nationalisation of the land was, for the socialists, to be considered as a vital part of the wider policy of taking all the means of production and exchange into common ownership.

Social reform was an area in which socialists in the late nineteenth century put forward an enormous number of policy proposals, though here there is much less continuity with early periods than there is on the question of land. Socialists in the early part of the nineteenth century did not develop any substantial social reform programme. There are a number of possible reasons which might be suggested for this lack of detailed concern on this issue. First, the early nineteenth century was a period in which the state apparatus, at both central and local level, was relatively undeveloped. On a practical level, therefore, state machinery did not present itself as the most obvious avenue for promoting the welfare of the people. Furthermore, the machinery which did exist was in the control of a parliamentary and local government system dominated by aristocratic and manufacturing interests. Secondly, in terms of the experience which the mass of the population had of government intervention in this area, the Poor Law Amendment Act of 1834 provoked bitter resentment and hardly served as an encouraging model. Thirdly, there are reasons which stem from the theory of socialism in this early period. This is particularly true of Owenite theory, which viewed partial measures of social reform as leaving the fundamental characteristics of the environment unaltered. In Owen's view socialism could only be established in communities based on the co-operative principle. There were, however, people subscribing to Owenite views who, as we have seen, were in favour of parliamentary action but here political reform was seen as the prime objective. Social reform could therefore only be achieved through a reformed system of government. Some of the problems which socialists faced on social reform may be illustrated by a brief discussion of attitudes towards education. For many socialists, particularly those who were 'moral force' Chartists, education was a necessary condition for the spread of democracy. However, much of the available education provision was provided by the middle class and overtly concerned to promote acceptance of the existing political and economic system. Voluntary organisations such as the Mechanics Institute and the Society for the Diffusion of Useful Knowledge directed their attention towards the adult working class, particularly the skilled artisan. The British Society and the National Society – with the help of government grants after 1833 – aimed to provide a highly disciplined, moral education for working-class children. In this situation the activities of socialists were directed towards developing separate educational organisations, particularly for adults, rather than seeking extension or reform of existing provision.

By the late nineteenth century socialists were faced with a much more developed state apparatus, increased democracy, the decline of patronage and corruption, and increased state intervention along lines which provided a cause for optimism about future developments in improving social welfare. Social reform in this period was much more central to socialist proposals, as indeed it was to Liberals and Conservatives. There was by no means unanimous support, since the Socialist League was formally opposed to parliamentary gradualism and the SDF, though including many social reforms in its programme, still tended to regard these as 'palliatives'. The most extensive support and proposals for social reform came from the Fabians and the ILP, both of which organisations regarded the extension of existing governmental services and activities as the means by which socialist welfare objectives should be achieved. Central to these policy proposals was the development of the activities of local authorities rather than those of national government. Municipal socialism was attractive not only in practical administrative terms but also in terms of the opportunities it offered for active participation and democratic control. Thus municipal control was suggested not only for land but for education, gas, water, and electricity, care of the aged, the sick, child welfare, provision of public works for the unemployed, the liquor trade and licensing, milk supply, housing and hospitals. There was also support for the extension of municipal trading enterprises and public works departments. Proposals for national control of services was largely restricted to those which had 'national' rather than 'local' characteristics, such as the railways and the mines. These social reform policies were part of the demand for the 'national minimum' – a standard of living, not merely an income, below which no-one should be allowed to fall. The 'national minimum' embraced conditions at work, maintenance of a healthy environment, housing and educational standards and protection against the consequences of unemployment, old age, poverty and ill-health. There was widespread support among socialists for all these measures, particularly for the provision of a universal, free system of education at primary, secondary and higher levels, for free school meals and for the breakup of the existing poor law and the provision of old-age pensions. Since the poor law was the main agent for social welfare provision in the nineteenth century and excited debate among all shades of opinion, it will be useful to consider these proposals in a little more detail. The proposal to take the aged out of the poor law system by providing pensions was by no means confined to socialists but, in this debate, the Fabians and the ILP favoured old-age pensions as a right at the age of sixty-five and were completely opposed to either voluntary or compulsory insurance contributions as a method of financing these or any other form of income maintenance, for example unemployment and sickness insurance. Voluntary insurance would never produce the necessary finance while compulsory contributions would lower the incomes of the working class. Socialists therefore favoured non-contributory pensions financed out of progressive taxation with a much higher rate of taxation on unearned incomes. Opposition to the poor law centred on criticism of the deterrence principle of poor relief, the non-democratic nature of the Boards of Guardians and the inability of a single administrative body to deal with the complexities of the problem of poverty. The complete breakup of the poor law was the only solution to these problems. The stigma of pauperism should be removed by recognition of the social causes of poverty, and this could not be achieved by reforming the existing system. Unemployment should therefore be dealt with through the provision of public works, while those whose poverty was the result of other causes should be dealt with by specialised committees of the local authorities. Thus, the needs of the sick poor would be met by the Public Health Committee, those of poor children by the Education Committee, the insane and mentally ill by the Asylums Committee and the aged by the Pensions Committee. These recommendations formed the substance of the Minority Report of the Royal Commission on the Poor Law (1909). This was largely the work of Sydney and Beatrice Webb but the ILP proposals on the poor law were substantially the same.

In terms of policy proposals there does appear to be a high degree of unanimity among socialists at the turn of the century. The major differences focus not on the objectives themselves but on the attitudes which should be taken towards the legislation being passed by Conservative and Liberal governments – whether or not such legislation should be opposed or supported as a positive step towards the objectives. In this respect the Fabians were frequently more optimistic and more inclined to support developments, particularly in local government, than were members of the socialist organisations. There were differences also in the kinds of arguments put forward to support these policies. The Fabian Society increasingly distanced itself from both the moral imperative of these proposals and from its own more abstract theory. Under the influence particularly of Sydney Webb and his wife Beatrice, née Potter (1858–1943), Fabian proposals were based on detailed, empirical, historical enquiries into particular areas, giving the impression of being more concerned with the efficiency of administrative arrangements in specific services rather than the overall structure of society; an impression which, not without justification, gives rise to the charge that they were more interested in piecemeal social engineering than the creation of a socialist society.

IMPACT ON LEGISLATION

The task of assessing the influence of socialists on legislation in the period up to the Great War is made extremely difficult by the fact that their formal political role – occupation of central or local government office – is, for most of the century, virtually non-existent. Although the nineteenth century witnessed a number of reforms which were approved of by socialists these were passed by Liberal or Conservative governments Thus by the turn of the century advances had been made in the provision of public health, working-class housing and education; tighter legal controls over conditions and hours of work were brought into operation; the franchise had been considerably extended and the legal status of trade unions had been made clearer. At local level there had been extensions of municipal control over lighting, sewage and drainage and the provision of recreational facilities such as parks, libraries and museums. The authorities themselves had been reformed and modernised. This is not to suggest that by the end of the nineteenth century the major problems of industrial society had been solved by an unconscious movement towards state socialism. Though this view characterises much of Fabian literature, the response of socialists generally was to point to such examples as demonstrating the necessity for state intervention and its feasibility, whilst criticising the partial nature and subsequent ineffectiveness of legislation which was not grounded on socialist principles. Liberal and Conservative reforms were thus welcomed only in the sense that they demonstrated both the need for more drastic and far-reaching change and the inability of either party to provide either the necessary analysis of the problems or the means of dealing with them. Thus Britain in the late nineteenth century had failed to deal with the massive problem of unemployment and the grinding poverty of so many of its inhabitants: malnutrition, ill-health, inadequate housing, were constant features of working-class life, particularly in urban areas. The system of education provided neither for the needs of children nor for the demands of a complex industrial society. The sick and aged were subject either to the punitive poor law system or dependent on the whims of charity. Similarly in industrial life socialists identified continuing abuses of the working population in wages, safety and hours of work. They saw themselves not merely as demanding 'more of the same' in terms of legislation but as using existing practice as evidence for the need for a different kind of society.

It might be argued that such self-perception had less and less validity as the century progressed – that whereas socialism was totally extra-parliamentary in the early nineteenth century and the different nature of their demands was clear, by the turn of the century the gradual, reformist, parliamentary socialists found it increasingly difficult to establish a practical difference between themselves and progressives in the Liberal party. This later period had the additional complexity that socialists found their political voice largely through organised labour, which raises the question as to how far legislation which had the support of labour also had the support of socialists within the labour movement. To interpret socialism as moving from a clearly identifiable extra-parliamentary movement to one which accepted gradual legislative change does not solve the problem of assessing the influence of socialists in working-class politics. In the earlier part of the century neither Chartism, nor the co-operative movement, nor the trade unions can be accurately described as socialist so that, even where working-class agitation could be shown to be influential, the question of socialist influence still remains to be answered.

Such influence was, at most, indirect. The socialist voice within working-class movements made a contribution to the way in which the political rulers perceived such movements in the 1830s and 1840s. That is, they contributed to demands which, if met, were seen as leading to the destruction of the social and political framework. Such a perception provoked several responses: first, one which sought to ameliorate the conditions of the working class through factory and mines legislation and to direct and control their sentiments through the extension of education: secondly, a response of firm opposition to change: a demand to assert the power of the established order; and last a reactionary response, a desire to turn back the clock and reassert the values of pre-industrial society. Legislation tended to reflect the first response tempered by the second, sometimes to the point of ineffectiveness, as proposals were 'watered down', with discretion replacing compulsion and central control giving way to local autonomy. It was in the decades after 1850 that greater concessions to working-class pressure were made, decades in which, as we have seen, socialist influence was at its lowest ebb. This period saw considerable extension of trade union rights, the extension of the franchise to the urban working class in 1867, stricter control over employers, more effective public health legislation and the beginnings of a state system of education. The retreat of socialism coincides with a change in the demands of working-class organisations, the demand to be included in the system rather than to transform it. This is not to suggest, however, that the working class had become a passive and malleable mass. The Hyde Park riots preceding the 1867 Reform Act, though neither as bloody nor as violent as those earlier in the nineteenth century, provoked a good deal of fear. At least as far as Disraeli was concerned fear of the consequences of not making concessions appears to have been greater than fear of the consequences of meeting the demand for reform. The Reform League, which had organised the demonstrations, though not the violence, drew a great deal of its support from the trade unions. This support was not based on socialist ideology but on the necessity of the vote to pursue the narrower economic interests of the trade unions. Not until the demonstrations of the unemployed in London in 1886 and the industrial troubles of 1889 were socialists again directly involved in popular agitation. Even then the numbers were small but the relevance of socialism to working-class politics had begun to be demonstrated. It was a relevance which increasingly came to be demonstrated through representative political action rather than in extra-parliamentary activity and one which included a comprehensive programme for legislative reform. It was in local government that socialists first began to make their presence felt. The Local Government Act of 1888 modernised the administrative machinery of local government, creating sixty-two Adminstrative Counties and sixty County Boroughs, all of which were to be controlled by elected bodies. This establishment of local democracy opened the door for socialists to take an active part in municipal politics, particularly in London where the LCC was established in 1889. The Parish Councils Act of 1894 also made a considerable breach in the domination of rural local government by the landed interest and offered a further possibility for political activity, albeit fairly limited. Substantial advances were made in the local provision of housing, public works and education by the newly created authorities. Though credit for these achievements must be shared between progressive Liberals, radicals and socialists, local politics provided an important arena in which to demonstrate 'practical' socialism. Similar avenues for participation had also been opened up by the 1870 Education Act and the locally-elected school boards for the provision of elementary education were dominated in many areas by socialists and labour interests.

Though the specific influence of the Fabians in London government has been questioned, the LCC was regarded by the Salisbury administration of 1895 as a hotbed of 'socialist' activity. 'Socialist' here is used in the broad sense, common in the 1890s, to refer to all extensions of collective provision, but the reaction of the Conservative government gives some indication of the opportunities for change which local government presented. It was an opportunity which Salisbury was determined to limit, at least in the capital, and in 1899 the London Government Act decentralised the LCC by creating ten boroughs. It was a measure which was violently opposed by the Progressive Party in London, the exception being the executive of the Fabian Society whose original opposition had turned to qualified support for the Act.

This was not the only occasion on which the Fabians found themselves out of step with socialist opinion as they reacted to legislation. A more serious difference of opinion arose concerning A. J. Balfour's Education Act of 1902. In the period before the Act local councils had entered the education field through the Technical Instruction Act of 1889 and several attacks had been mounted on elementary school boards for wasteful use of public funds. A proposal was put forward by the Conservative government to transfer responsibility for elementary education to the local authorities. This was violently opposed by the majority of socialist opinion as an attempt to close down an important area of their local influence. The Fabians were the exception[33] with Webb in particular favouring a streamlined administrative structure for education by transferring responsibility to the local authority. Webb, who was Chairman of the LCC Technical Education Board, played an important part in framing the subsequent Education Act which designated County and County Borough Councils as Local Education Authorities and gave them power to provide both elementary education and education other than elementary. Though Webb's personal influence here may have been considerable it could hardly be said to represent socialist opinion. Socialists could exploit some of the possibilities of local politics but without a significant parliamentary presence their role in national legislation was limited to one of reacting, with little effect, to legislation already passed. Such a judgement also applies to the Fabian Society. Although in figures like Sydney Webb and his wife Beatrice it possessed individuals commanding great respect in government circles, the Fabian Society only appears to have exercised influence where its prescriptions were compatible with policy decisions already embarked on.

At the General Election of 1906 the Labour Representation Committee (LRC) won 29 seats, with another MP joining their ranks shortly afterwards, and the name 'Labour Party' was adopted. The Liberal party won 377 seats with an overall majority of 84 and embarked upon an unprecedented programme of legislation. Any judgement on the extent to which socialists influenced such a programme is fraught with difficulties. First, by no means all of the members of the parliamentary Labour party were socialists – only 18 out of the 30 members. Secondly, although there was a pact between the Liberal party and the LRC prior to the election, the Liberal government was not dependent on Labour support in the House of Commons. Thirdly, the Liberals had their own ideological framework through which to develop legislative action and a number of influential members of the Liberal party were committed to radical change. Thus the Labour party might be seen as no more than a pressure group within parliament and the socialists as a pressure group within the Labour party.

In the area of social reform the Liberal government passed legislation which could not fail to gain the support of socialists in the Labour party but there is little which could be attributed to their initiative. Thus the Old-Age Pensions Act, the Children's Act, medical inspection for schoolchildren and the changes in taxation were all approved of by the socialists. In previous years they had made considerable contributions to the debates on these questions outside parliament. In this sense we can see socialists as having taken an active but not necessarily decisive role in creating a climate of opinion in which such legislation became a possibility. In parliament, however, the Liberals always seem to have been one step ahead and only the 1906 Education (Provision of Meals) Act, which gave local authorities the power to provide school meals out of the rates, came about as a result of a Bill introduced by a Labour member. Indeed, in one significant area where socialist opinion was opposed to Liberal social reform that opposition was easily over-ridden. This was the issue of social insurance introduced by Lloyd George in 1911. The basis of the Labour party's opposition was that a contributory insurance scheme represented a regressive form of taxation on wage-earners which would bring financial benefit only to the better-off sections of the working class and intensify the problems of low wages. The working class was therefore being asked to bear a financial burden which ought to be spread across the community as a whole. In introducing this provision, Lloyd George not only ignored the specific opposition to contributory insurance but also the proposals to break up the poor law, contained in the Minority Report of 1909, which had firm socialist support.

The Labour party had much greater success in the area of industrial policy, particularly on the question of the legal rights of trade unions. The 1906 Trades Dispute Act restored the legal immunity of trade unions and effectively reversed the Taff Vale judgment. This was followed by the Workmen's Compensation Act of 1906, the introduction of the eight-hour day for coalminers in 1908 and minimum wage legislation for miners in 1912. Another success for organised labour came in 1913 when the Trade Union Act of that year legalised the use of trade union funds for political purposes where a majority of members voted to do so – though individual trade unionists were allowed to opt out of paying any political levy. This Act was passed as a result of a judgment by the Law Lords in 1909 on an action brought by a railway employee, W. V. Osborne. The Osborne judgment had ruled that a compulsory political levy by trade unions was ultra vires, a decision which had robbed the Labour party of its financial base. The effects of that decision had been mitigated to some extent by the introduction of payments for MPs in 1911 – a long-standing demand of the trade unions and socialists – but the 1913 Act indicates the extent to which the Liberal party was anxious to appease the trade union movement.

It would appear then that the Liberal government was most susceptible to pressure from the Labour party on specific industrial issues. This is unsurprising since the Liberals had traditionally enjoyed a close relationship with the trade unions. The establishment and growth of the LRC and then the Labour party had considerably weakened this relationship and the long-term threat of a separate party representing organised labour was more important than the growth of a socialist party. The period before the First World War was also marked by widespread and violent industrial unrest and Liberal action on trade union legislation may be viewed as a response to this, particularly as an attempt to gain the support of the most powerful and highly organised unions.

Is the judgement of socialist influence before the First World War to be almost wholly negative? The answer is that any judgement must bear in mind the domination of popular politics by the Liberal and Conservative parties and the problems which this presented for a form of socialism committed to gradual reform through the parliamentary process. The need for independent political action was one which had to be demonstrated and then the relevance of socialist ideas to that political action had to be proved. Though the first task had been largely achieved by 1906 the second had only just begun. The mixture of socialism by legislation and a trade union movement anxious to use legislation only to provide a legal framework for the free operation of collective bargaining was bound to prove volatile. Nevertheless from 1906 onwards the socialists made steady progress as the Labour party gradually committed itself to more and more socialist objectives – a more equal distribution of income, public ownership of monopolies, nationalisation of the railways, canals and land, and a state medical service. A moderate form of socialism this may have been, and one which fell a long way short of a coherent ideology, but it was through such socialism that the Labour party began to form a distinct political identity which has proved durable at least until the present time, in spite of the diverse elements it contains.

REFERENCES AND NOTES

1. The following discussion owes much to Berki, R. N. (1975) *Socialism*, Chapter 2. J. M. Dent: London
2. J. F. C. Harrison 'A New View of Mr Owen' in Pollard, S. and Salt, J. (eds) (1971) *Robert Owen, Prophet of the Poor*. Macmillan: London, p. 1
3. Robert Owen (1972) *A New View of Society* (introduction by J. Saville). Macmillan: London, p. 27
4. Robert Owen (1972) p. 34
5. Maurice, J. *Life of F. D. Maurice* quoted in Beer, M. (1953) *A History of British Socialism*, vol. II. George Allen and Unwin: London, p. 182
6. J. M. Ludlow (1848) *The Great Partnership* quoted in H. Pelling (ed.) (1954) *The Challenge of Socialism*. Adam and Charles Black: London, p. 88
7. F. D. Maurice quoted in Christensen, T. (1962) *Origin and History of Christian Socialism 1848–1854*. Universitets forlaget I: Aarhus, p. 29

8. Hyndman, H. M. (1911) *The Record of An Adventurous Life.* Macmillan: London, p. 282

9. Hyndman, H. M. (1911) p. 337

10. Hyndman, H. M. (1922) *The Economics of Socialism. Marx made Easy.* Grant Richards: London, p. 102

11. Morris, W. (1885) *The Workers' Share of Art* quoted in Briggs, A. (ed.) (1973) *William Morris: Selected Writings and Designs.* Penguin: Harmondsworth, p. 143

12. Morris, W. (1883) Letter to T. C. Horsfall in Briggs (1973) p. 150

13. Morris, W. (1883) in Briggs (1973) p. 150

14. Davidson, T. quoted in Wolfe, W. (1975) *From Radicalism to Socialism 1881–1889.* Yale University Press: New Haven and London, p. 155

15. *Fabian Essays* (1889) (sixth edition with introduction by A. Briggs) (1962). George Allen and Unwin: London, p. 212

16. *Fabian Essays* (1889) p. 214

17. *Fabian Essays* (1889) p. 228

18. *Fabian Essays* (1889) p. 46

19. *Fabian Essays* (1889) pp. 55

20. *Fabian Essays* (1889) pp. 66

21. *Fabian Essays* (1889) pp. 66–67

22. Pease, E. R. (1963) *The History of the Fabian Society* (introduction by M. Cole). Frank Cass: London, p. 102. First published 1918

23. *Fabian Essays* (1889) p. 90

24. *Nation* 30 March 1907 quoted in Pierson, S. (1979) *British Socialists: The Journey from Fantasy to Politics.* Harvard University Press: Cambridge, Mass. and London

25. Pease, E. R. (1963) p. 111

26. Hardie, J. K. (1974) *From Serfdom to Socialism* (introduction by R. E. Dowse). Harvester Press: Brighton, p. 35. First published 1907, Allen and Unwin: London

27. Hardie, J. K. (1974) p. 44

28. Blatchford, R. (1895) *Merrie England.* Clarion Newspapers Limited, Walter Scott Limited: London, p. 15

29. Harry Quelch, *Report of the XXII Annual Conference of the SDF 1902*, quoted in Beer, M. (1953) *A History of British Socialism*, vol. II. George Allen and Unwin: London, p. 273

30. McBriar, A. M. (1962) *Fabian Socialism and English Politics 1884–1918.* Cambridge University Press: London, p. 311

31. Harrison, R. (1965) *Before the Socialists*. Routledge and Kegan Paul: London; University of Toronto Press: Toronto, p. 7
32. Fabian Tract Number 7 (1908) 7th edn revised, p. 6
33. See Fabian Tract Number 106 *The Education Muddle and the Way Out*.

Chapter five
NEW LIBERALISM

POLITICAL THEORY

The term 'New Liberalism' is used to describe significant developments in liberal theory and practice in the last two decades of the nineteenth and first decade of the twentieth centuries which not only adapted the traditional concerns of liberalism to changing economic, social and political circumstances but also provided a dynamic framework in which those circumstances could be analysed and acted upon. The political theory of New Liberalism found its most articulate expression in the works of T. H. Green, D. G. Ritchie, L. T. Hobhouse and J. A. Hobson, and was not simply a restatement of long-standing ideals but a major contribution to the liberal tradition, envisaging a positive role for the State in the amelioration of social problems and the creation of the good society. One should beware, however, of regarding such a development as a clean break with the past or a sudden change of direction as is often implied by referring to New Liberalism as 'collectivism' and traditional liberal theory as 'individualism'. To see developments in such clearly antithetical terms is to ignore the constant interaction between theory and practice and to see liberalism as a static rather than as a continuously developing philosophy. The terms 'individualism' and 'collectivism' were a vital part of the political debate in the period 1880–1914 but this dichotomy is often confusing as an explanation of developments in political theory since there are elements of both individualism and collectivism in New Liberalism and in the works of Bentham and J. S. Mill. Caution is necessary in the use of categories and typologies, particularly those which draw attention away from the continuities of the liberal tradition of discourse.

Many of the concerns of New Liberalism can be found not only in the theories of Bentham and Mill but also in the more general movement of ideas in Victorian society. The obligation to promote a moral society found its expression in numerous campaigns for moral reform, from temperance to anti-vivisection, which cut across party lines. Existing legislation in the areas of poor relief, public health and factory conditions bear witness to the use of state power, not merely for regulation but for the positive improvement of the individual and society. Moral questions, centring on the problem of the relationship between the individual and the State and their respective responsibilities, dominated mid-nineteenth-century thought. Liberalism had always been a doctrine of reform but the long-standing targets of the aristocracy and government dominated by group interests were increasingly replaced by the problems of a complex industrial society. New Liberalism was a response to the failure of existing liberal theory to provide a framework for reform in these changed circumstances. Though there is no necessary connection between utilitarianism and *laissez-faire*, or between J. S. Mill's liberalism and *laissez-faire*, these theories did leave themselves open to an interpretation which justified economic competition and the minimum of social regulation. Though there had been some movement in Liberal thought away from the notion of indefeasible individual rights, in general it still maintained a view of the individual as the ultimate moral, economic and political reality. The task of New Liberalism was to formulate a 'comprehensive and conscious theory of social life which could yet retain its specific liberal characteristics'.[1] The formulation was often complex, drawing as it did on orthodox liberal theory, idealist philosophy and the evolutionary theories which so dominated all late-Victorian thought. Before moving to a more detailed consideration of the content of this theory it is necessary to offer some explanation of idealism, particularly as formulated by T. H. Green.

T. H. Green (1836–82) was tutor and later Professor of Moral Philosophy at Balliol College, Oxford and is often credited with the major responsibility for New Liberal thought. Although his influence has been questioned, what can be said is that, while the works of Hobhouse and Hobson show fundamental differences from Green's approach, his philosophy had a profound influence on the vocabulary of political debate. That is, many of the questions which Green raised, and the concepts which he developed in answer to them, were an important element in directing the questions and answers of those who followed.

Green was a devoutly religious man with a highly developed sense of public duty, who saw in the empiricist tradition of British philosophy, and particularly in the development of evolutionary theories, an attempt to construct a science of ethics. Such a scientific approach to moral questions was, he believed, doomed to failure since if men were regarded simply as receptive beings, as natural objects existing among other natural objects and subject to the same laws, then there could be no question of moral responsibility. The laws of evolution or any other laws of nature are merely descriptive and from them can be derived no grounds on which to decide what men ought to do. Utilitarianism was similarly criticised even though Green recognised that, as a doctrine of reform and a check on injustice, much had been achieved by it. However, the theory contained within it elements which might act as a block to further reform since it could not provide a guide or rationale for those acts performed for the sake of duty to others which form the framework of social reform. Utilitarianism was in danger of changing from a doctrine of practical reform into a theoretical justification for selfishness and complacency.

Green sought to establish a theory of ethics and of political obligation which would not be open to empirical refutation and which would tell us not only how men do act but how they ought to act. In doing so he drew heavily on the philosophy of Kant and Hegel, the idealist tradition which was alien to British philosophy, but also on the liberal values of men like Bright. The processes by which Green reached his political theory are complex and all that can be done in the context of an exposition of New Liberalism is to indicate some of the recurring themes in his thought. Green argues that what sets man apart from merely natural phenomena is the possession of self-consciousness or reason. The exercise of this reason shows man his limitations but also makes him aware of his potentiality as a rational, moral being. It is this awareness of the gap between what a man is and what he might be which is the driving force of progress. The full realisation of this potential is the end or purpose of human history. In ethical terms reason also demonstrates that just as each individual is striving to achieve his real self he is likewise conscious of others so striving, and he must conceive of 'a permanent well-being in which the permanent well-being of others is included . . . Some sort of community founded on such unity of self-consciousness, on such a capacity for a common idea of permanent good, must be pre-supposed in any groupings of men from which the society we know can have been developed.'[2]

Morality, and the concepts of rights, duties and obligation, have no meaning outside society and society has its basis in reason. The obligation to pursue the interests of others is not derived from contract or utility or prudence but from the exercise of self-conciousness. The distinctions between the individual and society, between self-regarding and other regarding acts, which result from atomistic views of society, are thus a fiction. Social institutions are a product of this consciousness; they exist to

> render it possible for a man to be freely determined by the idea of a possible satisfaction of himself, instead of being driven this way and that by external forces, and thus they give reality to the capacity called the will; and they enable him to realise his reason is his idea of self-perfection, by acting as a member of a social organisation in which each contributes to the better being of all the rest.[3]

According to Green, a study of the history of institutions shows that the modern State is the most effective means of giving expression to the development of the common good. We obey the State not because of its coercive power but because it increases our capacity to move towards self-realisation. State activity is not an encroachment on individual freedom but an essential element in that freedom. 'Freedom' here has undergone a redefinition. It is no longer absence of restraint but a positive power.

A man is free in so far as he realises his real self – that dictated by his reason rather than passion or appetite. This 'real self' cannot be realised apart from that of his fellows, 'the common good'. Just as the individual recognises this power in others, so it is recognised by other moral agents and this is the basis of 'rights'; they are powers necessary to the fulfilment of men as moral beings. Such fulfilment cannot be realised by individuals except in so far as they promote it in others. Rights cannot, therefore, exist apart from a society in which a common good is recognised. The State comes into being in order to guarantee these rights through recognition by law, its purpose being to create the framework for a moral life and to remove obstacles to the development of such a life.

There are certain problems here in that Green seems to have created the possibility of a profoundly illiberal State, one in which the individual is entirely subordinate to society and social institutions with no area of life which lies outside the province of the law. Green's answers to such charges may be stated as follows. First, no actual State corresponds to the 'ideal' and therefore where the 'common good' demands it, reform and ultimately resistance are permissible. Such resistance is not justifiable, however, if it leads to the destruction of the State. This would be to create a general loss of freedom which would not be to the 'common good'. Secondly, he insists that the freedom of which he speaks can only be realised in individuals. The ultimate standard of worth is an ideal of personal worth and the nation, society and the State are delusive abstractions if seen as ends in themselves. Thirdly, he finds the limitation of the law in the nature of morality itself. The good man is one who freely wills certain objectives rather than others and thus moral duties cannot be enforced. Law can only regulate acts and not the motives for those acts and indeed it may actually be destructive of the development of moral autonomy. 'The state has no positive moral function of making its members better: it has the negative moral function of removing the obstacles which prevent them from making themselves better.'[4] Although the practical proposals for reform which Green derived from his political theory were extremely moderate, and consistent with limited state interference, the possibility of deriving from them an authoritarian State led other progressive liberals to seek a more consistently liberal basis for social reform.

L. T. Hobhouse (1864–1929), while acknowledging the contribution made by Green to the development of liberal thought, attacked idealist metaphysics for its illiberal tendencies: 'in laying down a certain kind of life as expressing the real will of the individual, the ground is prepared for the argument that in the compulsion of the individual to lead such a life there is no interference with his real will. He is supposed to be merely unable to judge for himself.'[5] Though idealist philosophy offered the possibility of an escape from the individualism which set men against one another, and an explanation of progress, in its conception of human society as the unfolding of a spiritual principle, it nevertheless encouraged complacency and discouraged the constant examination of actual experience which Hobhouse sees as fundamental to social reform and the preservation of liberty. In the climate of the late-Victorian period such examination meant coming to terms with evolutionary theory. After the publication of Darwin's *Origin of Species* (1859) the view that evolution was the key to understanding human society became firmly established.

There were, however, certain problems inherent in any attempt to weld together the ethical elements of idealism with the empirical, scientific approach of evolutionary theory in order to produce a liberal theory of social reform. Not the least of these was that understanding social development as the outcome of 'laws' of evolution tended to eliminate choice and human agency as factors in social progress. The concept of evolution in the hands of Spencer and his followers had also become a theory which justified competitive individualism and the minimum of state intervention. On this view it was the struggle for survival and the free play of instinctive forces which was the driving force of social development, a self-adjusting process which required no external political direction. Evolution could then be interpreted as underwriting classical political economy.

In spite of these difficulties it was to the concept of evolution that Hobhouse and then J. A. Hobson (1858–1940) turned in search of a scientific basis for their ethical theories, particularly to the 'organic' concept of society. The organic concept of society was by no means new. Indeed, in Conservative thought and in some versions of idealism it was associated with opposition to change in society since such change would upset the natural balance and harmony of the organism. D. G. Ritchie (1853–1903) had already cleared much of the ground in developing a dynamic and purposive concept of society in a theory which he termed 'Idealist Evolutionism'. Ritchie accepted the idealist view of human rationality as directed towards an ethical end and freedom as self-realisation, but also found in Darwin's theory of evolution a biological explanation of the social nature of individuals and the common good. He warns that biological concepts may be misleading when applied to human society: 'an uncritical use of them in a more complex material means a constant risk of mistaking metaphors for scientific laws'.[6] Although man is a biological organism subject to natural forces, he is also possessed of consciousness, he can think and reflect and, within limits, can direct natural forces. Natural selection in human society is not then a merely mechanical process outside human agency, it is the product of reason and consciousness – a process which Ritchie calls rational selection. Nor is such a process simply the unfolding of an ideal, but a constant interplay between visions of the future, experience of the present and reflection on the past. Darwinian theory explains this process by showing how each species has come to be what it is by pursuing its own good – the structure and habits of an organism are to be explained by the purpose which they serve. Thus the organic concept of society shows us that:

> Morality to begin with means those feelings and acts and habits which are advantageous to the community. Morality comes to mean the conscious and deliberate adoption of those feelings and acts and habits which are advantageous to the welfare of the community and reflection makes it possible to alter the conception of what the community is whose welfare is to be considered.'

Right and wrong now appear as whatever helps or hinders the good of society and the ethical end for the individual must be a social end – the common good.

This consciousness of interdependence in pursuing a common good finds its most developed expression in the organised State which, by deliberate and conscious action, can minimise the waste of the struggle for existence. There is, then, no antithesis between the State and the individual and science demonstrates that individuals, as human beings with rights and duties rather than as mere animals, can only be understood by reference to society. In judging the rights of individuals or in evaluating social institutions we must judge from the point of view of society as a whole. The creation of the best life of the individual is the purpose of the State; the best life can only be realised in an organised society and that means in the State. This, then, presented a justification for collective action on social ills and for active social reform.

Hobhouse and Hobson developed further this fusion of idealism and evolutionism and the organic concept of society is central to their theory. However, the question of the relationship between the parts and the whole of the organism, the individual and society, continued to pose problems for a liberal theory of the State and of law. Hobhouse believed that evolution demonstrated the development of harmony in social life and that progress consists of greater organisation and co-operation. This in turn is a result of the development of 'mind', that self-conscious intelligence through which men become aware of their essential one-ness. Co-operation and awareness of a common good are products of rationality and therefore there is no conflict between the whole and the parts. Rational consideration leads us to see that self-devolopment includes taking into account the development of the good of others and to realise that 'The true conception of an organic society is one in which the best life of each man is felt to be bound up with the best life of his fellow citizen.'[8] It is this which brings about progress in evolution, and collectivism is the attempt to shape social customs and institutions in this spirit. Collectivism then becomes an extension of human morality and the State is seen as an advanced ethical institution, the purpose of which is the maintenance and improvement of life.

Hobhouse always firmly insisted on the role of conscious thought and action in this evolutionary process and also that the social organism was not some mystical entity with a separate existence. On this he appears to differ from Hobson though he too is constantly aware of the danger of elevating the State to an end in itself. The dominant idea is rather that of a reciprocal relationship between the individual and the State which may best be appreciated by a discussion of the concept of rights. Hobhouse claims that the moral right of an individual is simply a condition of the full development of his personality as a moral being. The community also has a moral right to the maintenance of the common good which is best furthered by the abilities of individual members to make the best of themselves. This then means that there is no necessary conflict between the community and the individual. It also appears that only those activities which positively contribute to the common good can be considered to be right: not simply those which foster self-development but those which actively further the development of others. Though there is an unconvincing circularity in this argument, the concept of rights here may not be as restrictive as it first appears. It is the task of the social reformer continually to extend the notion of the common good, and thus the area of 'rights', in pursuing the aim of social harmony. Indeed it is in terms of 'rights' that Hobhouse formulated a demand for minimum income and the provision of education and health care.

Hobson, while sharing the notion of rights as socially defined, develops the notion of 'social utility' as paramount in marking the limits of those rights. Social utility is an objective standard – a social ideal constructed to accord with 'human facts' and 'human possibilities' – which includes both the ethical and physical aspects of life. Hobson claimed that the common good was to be the test of rights but also that the content of the common good could be empirically established. This indeed was to be the task of a science of welfare.

The danger here is that the individual may become entirely subordinate to social ends and, furthermore, ends which are defined by experts in the science of welfare. Indeed, in his discussion of 'organic democracy' Hobson states that the organic concept of society destroys the idea of natural individual rights as the basis of democracy. Democracy is to be justified not on the grounds that each man is the best judge of his own interests but in terms of the functional necessity of each cell of the organism to transmit information to the cerebral centre where policy is formulated. The right of veto and protest is essential to achieving a proper balance and a healthy organism – the cells must not be forced to do what they are not capable of doing. However: 'Understand that these rights of members and their cells are not in any sense a qualification or denial of the truth that the good of the organism as a whole is the absolute criterion of conduct and may, in extreme cases, require the complete sacrifice of an organ and its cells.'[9]

This delicate juggling of the traditional liberal value of individuality and the need for a collectivist concept of society is characteristic of New Liberalism. It is, moreover, a delicate balance which is preserved only at the cost of considerable ambiguity, whether it is expressed in terms of a 'real will' by Green, or supported by the organic concept of society derived from evolutionary theory. On the one hand, the repeated stress on the voluntary nature of morality and self-development as the touchstone for limiting state action appears to be a reformulation of liberal individualism, justified in terms of the contribution which it makes to the good of society as a whole. On the other hand, the abandonment of the distinction between self-regarding and other-regarding acts, and the attempts to break down the antithesis between the individual and society, seem to deprive the individual of any purely personal sphere. It is a problem which was not adequately resolved in theoretical terms in the writings of the New Liberals, but constant awareness, in those writings, of the tensions present in the task which they were undertaking is testimony to their claim to belong to the liberal tradition. It is a recurrent theme in the works of both Hobhouse and Hobson that a synthesis is needed between the values of the older liberalism and those of the new, and that the roots of their collectivist approach can be found in classical liberal theory. This does not appear to have been a purely instrumental exercise aimed at deriving the support of tradition for their views. The insistence on the ethical principles of social life and on the role of moral consciousness and human intellect in social progress led them to reject, not without some inconsistency and contradiction, both the elevation of the State as an end in itself and the deterministic conclusions of contemporary biological theory. The resultant ambiguities may perhaps be viewed as a strength rather than a weakness since they produced a degree of flexibility essential at a time of rapidly changing economic and social circumstances. A rationale for collective action on pressing social problems was the result of a deep concern for morality. How this concern revealed itself, striking a balance between the claims of the State and those of individuals, can only be fully appreciated by examining their practical proposals for legislative change.

PRACTICAL PROPOSALS

Theories may lead to many possibilities, indeed ambiguity appears to go hand in hand with a high level of generality. It is at the level of application to practical issues that we may more clearly discern the intentions of their authors. We are on firmer ground criticising consequences which were actually drawn out of the theory rather than those which might have been. This is not to suggest that theory and practice are divorced but to suggest that the two must be taken together.

Thus, although Green's metaphysics could open the door to the authoritarian State we find in his practical conclusions little which would not be endorsed by Cobden and Bright. The concept of self-realisation, for example, led him to a moderate view of the role of the State with regard to private property. Property was seen as essential to the individual's realisation of his real self, thus: 'Considered as representing the conquest of nature by the effort of free and variously gifted individuals, property must be unequal; and no less must it be so considered as a means by which individuals fulfil social functions.'[10] Green went on to defend the right of inheritance and bequest, and restricted his attack on property to the large-scale possession of land, the traditional Liberal target of the landowning aristocracy. Land being a limited commodity, large-scale private possession of it would deprive others of the opportunity to acquire the property needed for self-development. He was not critical of the capitalist system itself but saw the faults which existed as products of English history, the effects of which were gradually being overcome.

The preference for voluntary action in all spheres of life led Green to see some restrictions on the powers of the State. Its role is to maintain conditions favourable to a moral life and promote development of character by removing all hindrances. This could be seen as justifying extensive state interference depending on how widely 'hindrances' was interpreted; alternatively it could be interpreted to mean that by acting in a minimal way and leaving a wide area for voluntary action the State would effectively be removing hindrances to self-development. Unfortunately, Green put very little practical flesh on his theoretical skeleton but other idealist philosophers, notably Bernard Bosanquet, did so. Bosanquet (1848–1923) was a leading member of the Charity Organisation Society formed in 1869 to co-ordinate charitable activity and to develop a rigorous and effective method for discerning worthy cases for charitable help. Bosanquet held the view that poverty was caused by a defect in the character of the individual, a defect which state aid to the poor could only make more severe by rewarding idleness and undermining the impulse to self-development. State provision, particularly the Poor Law, was thus one of the hindrances to self-development and 'no conditions will raise the poor, if character is sacrificed, while hard conditions can be transformed with extraordinary rapidity by ceasing to demoralise the wage-earners'.[11] Thus it was possible to derive a minimal sphere of state action free from the concept of removal of hindrance as well as to derive a more positive role for the State as did Green himself.

Hobhouse and Hobson both denied the autonomous individual will on which Bosanquet's approach was founded, and in their organic concept of society they developed the social dimension of 'self-realisation'. What we must now do is to consider how, in the proposals which they put forward for social reform, they countered the self-reliance view of freedom expressed by the Charity Organisation Society and tried to avoid the charge of extreme state socialism.

Hobhouse begins by outlining a principle on which he feels all Liberals agree: that all liberty rests on restraint and that it is only through the establishment of law that individuals are freed from arbitrary aggression or coercion. An individual is thus free to pursue lines of action which do not cause injury to others, but such freedom is only possible by the imposition of restraints by law on his own behaviour and that of others. The organic concept of society demonstrates the interdependence of individuals, and experience of the social effects of action leads to a widening of the concept of injury. The next move was to include in the concept of injury, and thus in the areas of restraint essential to liberty, aspects of social life which had previously been excluded. The most fundamental of these is the inequality of income and wealth, which is at the root of inequality of opportunity for self-development and is therefore itself a restraint on liberty and a form of injury. Although the development of personality and moral sense is essentially voluntary, the scope for voluntary action is limited by many forms of coercion other than state action. By placing restraints on these forms of coercion the State is not decreasing but increasing the liberty of its members. True liberty rests in free consent but free consent is only possible where there is a large degree of equality between the parties: 'liberty without equality is a name of noble sound and squalid result'.[12] Existing legislation, particularly the Factory Acts protecting women and children, had recognised this principle but careful study of society revealed that 'modern economic conditions engender inequalities of wealth and foster forms of industrial organisation which constantly threaten to reduce political and civic equality to a meaningless form of words'.[13] Not only women and children, or the sick and the aged, but able-bodied adult males were placed in circumstances over which they had no control and therefore no responsibility. Bad housing, inadequate sanitation, lack of education, unemployment and poverty were therefore conditions in which the appeal to self-help had no meaning.

The sense in which equality is used here is not absolute equality but equality of opportunity: furnishing for each individual the conditions under which it will be possible for the individual not only to make the best of himself but also to make a positive contribution to the common good. It was an important premise of New Liberal proposals on social reform that legislative activity was not simply a transfer of goods and services from the advantaged to the disadvantaged, or a benefit for one class at the expense of another, but a benefit which improved the health of the whole organism. Thus Hobson defended 'equal opportunity' not only on moral grounds but also on economic grounds: 'The quantity of wealth available for distribution chiefly depends upon the stimulus afforded to the productive energies of man: this stimulus in its turn depends chiefly upon the opportunity open to every member of the community to do his best work.'[14]

What exactly did this mean in practical terms? In which areas of life should the equality-of-opportunity principle be applied? Hobson put forward a comprehensive list, though he stressed that this was not fixed, which included land, mobility, sources of energy, capital, security, justice and education. In terms of land, equal opportunity meant an equal chance of getting the use of a 'bit of land' and a 'fixed home in which to live', which required public ownership. Liberty also required freedom of movement and to be effective, to have not only the right to go but the means to do so, required a comprehensive network of public roads and the public ownership of the railways. Sources of energy should also be taken under public ownership since they were fundamental to the industrial processes of modern society. Private ownership would, in Hobson's view, open up the possibility of economic despotism on an intolerable scale. Credit or access to capital, for both the covering of emergencies and the development of business opportunities, was also seen as vital to the whole society. The danger was that control over industry would pass into the hands of financiers and therefore some form of public control was necessary. Even this did not go far enough, since no man can be free, who is not also secure. Private insurance had gone some way towards providing security but the competitive system was wasteful and resulted in high premiums to cover collection and administration. The responsibility of protecting members of society against the risks of modern life should therefore pass into the hands of government. Equality of access to the system of justice was, Hobson believed, a myth, though it was a requirement which all shades of opinion regarded as essential to liberty. No precise details were given but some form of public provision for legal expenses was put forward. Lastly, education – the 'opportunity of opportunities' for self-development – should be provided by the State. Although Hobson recognised the advances in state education achieved during the nineteenth century, provision still fell short of equal opportunity. Elementary education for the working class involved only the barest rudiments and access to any form of secondary education was extremely limited. Further provision of education was not simply a benefit for individuals but for society as a whole and should be provided not as a 'favour' or as an 'abstract right' but because it was socially important to society. Hobson and Hobhouse both argued that a programme of this nature was consistent with Liberal principles since liberty is not absence of restraint but the presence of opportunity. They also attempted to show such consistency by insisting that 'equal opportunity' must be understood in spiritual as well as material terms. An attempt was made to steer a middle course between seeing either individual character or material conditions as the sole determining factor but it was a course based on clearly formulated principles, the most important of which was the insistence on democratic control.

The discussion of democracy revolved around two basic issues. First, it was argued that the organic concept of society was wholly consistent with democracy and did not involve the political subordination of individuals to state bureaucracy: 'Democracy is not merely the government of a majority. It is rather the government which best expresses the community as a whole . . . .'[15] Secondly, they argued that democracy would act as a guarantee against the abuse of state power which could develop as a result of greatly extending its activities. The extension of the franchise from 1867 onwards had recognised the basic principle of democracy. Hobhouse and Hobson did not feel constrained to argue for recognition of the principle but rather sought ways of giving more substance to it by reform of the system of representation. The existing party system offered vigorous minorities the opportunity to wield undue influence in parliament. Proportional representation would secure a more representative parliament and guard against the undue favouring of particular interests. Proportional representation would not always present a clear expression of the will of the electorate and in such situations a direct appeal by referendum would be required. Hobson saw the first use of a referendum as being to bring about a reform of the House of Lords which, in 1909, was exercising its veto against the Liberal budget. A second chamber was regarded as essential as a safeguard against the dangers of a single unchecked chamber but its role should be advisory and consultative. He proposed that both Houses should have the power to call a referendum, thus making direct appeal to the electorate available to either one as a check on the other. Such extensions of democracy were seen as guarantees of virtue in public bodies whether virtue is understood as reflecting the will of the electorate or economic efficiency.

From the general arguments on equality of opportunity two more specific issues merit further consideration and these are the arguments on minimum income and on taxation. The idea of a minimum income was not the sole property of the New Liberals but it was central to their policies and was argued for on both moral and economic grounds. The purpose of the State is to secure the conditions under which morality can develop and without the conditions of self-maintenance, conditions which will make the exercise of responsibility a reality, moral development is stunted. Since the moral development of individuals cannot be separated from the development of the common good it follows that the community cannot remain indifferent to a situation in which some of its members do not have the physical basis on which to build moral characteristics. It is the duty of the community, therefore, to guarantee a minimum income. The existence of poverty also indicated a serious economic malaise since its causes could be identified as the waste of human power and the inequitable distribution of opportunities. The argument for redistribution on the equality-of-opportunity principle has already been examined and to this was now added the argument that unemployment, underemployment and misemployment reduced the amount of national wealth. A guaranteed minimum income would increase the power of consumption and the productive capacity of the population and, since it also involves an element of redistribution, would attack both the waste of human power and inequality.

The existing Poor Law did not meet the requirements of a minimum income on several grounds. First, it dealt only with absolute destitution, with pauperism and not poverty; it fulfilled no preventive function since relief could not be claimed by anyone with any income whatsoever, no matter how inadequate. Secondly, the income provided was not adequate to maintain a minimum standard of life, nor was there any 'right' to such a standard. Thirdly, it was an instrument deliberately designed to degrade the recipient: a system devised to deter the idler was applied to everyone who had recourse to relief. There does not seem to be any denial by the New Liberals that harsh treatment of the persistently idle was appropriate, it was rather that the existing system of poor relief and the inequitable distribution of income and wealth made it impossible to distinguish between those whose destitution was a result of force of circumstances and those in whom it was a defect of character. The solution was a guaranteed minimum standard of living for all citizens, which meant minimum wages, public provision of work for the unemployed, and pensions for the old and the sick. Any such proposal had to come to terms with the argument that such a guarantee would lead to the neglect of individual responsibility, the undermining of all incentive to work, and to the neglect of that most vital of virtues in late-Victorian England, thrift. The main thrust of the reply to this point has already been hinted at and can be summarised in the following way.

The independent existence which the self-reliance argument presupposed was a myth: 'study of industrial and social facts shows that this so-styled independence has no existence'.[16] What such a study revealed was that a great many of the working class were unable to provide for themselves and their families, and to save for their old age, because of the economic and social conditions under which they lived. The exhortation to self-help was therefore meaningless and the attempt to tackle the problem by moral regeneration of the poor was doomed to failure. There would be no decrease in incentives since in such a situation incentives cannot operate: 'the individual workman cannot put the machine straight. He is the last person to have any say in the market . . . He is not responsible for its ups and downs but has to pay for them.'[17] A policy of guaranteed minimum income would in fact begin to make sense of the notion of responsibility, since it would provide a secure foundation on which to build some hope of improvement, acting as a stimulus to thrift rather than paralysing it. Neither Hobhouse nor Hobson totally rejected the notions of incentives, responsibility and thrift but made an effort to put these values into a more meaningful frame of reference. Thus it was stressed that the 'function of the state is to secure conditions upon which its citizens are able to win by their own efforts all that is necessary to full civic efficiency'.[18] In other words the State's responsiblity was for a minimum over and above which individuals would bear responsibility. Similarly the concern to identify those who will not work was also present and it was claimed that such a policy would give a clear basis on which to judge those whose poverty was a result of wilful idleness. It is the right and duty of the individual to make the best of his opportunities and those who fail to do so may 'fairly suffer the penalty of being treated as a pauper or even, in an extreme case, as a criminal'.[19] Hobhouse also suggested that labour colonies should be provided in which such an individual should be forced to work until able to 'prove himself efficient enough in mind and body to stand the stress of individual competition'.[20]

There was one further objection to the 'national minimun' of which they were conscious and that was the charge that receipt of such a benefit would be demeaning since it was a form of charity, albeit administered by the State. This was countered by pointing out that since individuals were at the mercy of forces produced by social disorganisation it was not charity but justice which would be administered; since, on the organic concept of society, the whole organism is the beneficiary, payment of a minimum income is not analogous to a charitable act. The main argument, however, was that the claim to a minimum income was not a charge made by those without property on the propertied, but a right to a share in socially created property.

The theories of property, taxation and income put forward by the New Liberals were not monolithic but it is possible to identify certain basic principles on which there was widespread agreement. The first of these follows from the previous discussion of rights: there is no abstract individual right to property since all rights are socially created. The creation of wealth is only possible within a framework of social order backed by law – organised society is a precondition of the creation of wealth. The system of organised co-operation which expresses itself in the market and in the division of labour is a source of productive power. 'Society has, then, a natural claim upon property, on the ground that it is a maker of values of property.'[21] It is important to note here that society was not seen as the sole creator of values and New Liberalism attempted to identify both a social dimension of property and value and an individual dimension, preserving the private property necessary for the development of the individual while recognising the social property which is needed to support the life of the community. Thus a system of taxation based on the distinction between these two dimensions would not constitute an infringement of the rights of individuals or a process of confiscation but a move 'step by step from the wealth due to individual enterprise to the wealth that depends on its [society's] own collective progress, thus by degrees regaining the ownership of the fruits of its own collective work'.[22]

In a complex industrial society, however, the distinction between the social and individual elements in wealth is unlikely to be so clear. To this difficulty may be added the liberal requirements of recognition of individual differences, particularly motivation and incentive, which leads to the recognition of differential rewards. If absolute equality is rejected, what is to be the basis of the differences in remuneration over and above the minimum? Hobson suggested that rewards should be related to needs and that the individual should maintain the right of use over the income needed to support the best life of which he is capable. To keep any surplus above this would contribute to social waste and taxation of such surplus would not constitute a disincentive since the surplus would not make any contribution to the life of the individual. Hobhouse, on the other hand, wished to base such differentials on the amount necessary to stimulate and maintain the efficient exercise of useful functions, again any surplus above this constituting the social element. Such proposals are fraught with the difficulty of relying either on a centrally-planned system of reward which assumes a measure of agreement on 'needs' or 'useful functions', or on the mechanism of the market which has produced those inequalities which constitute the problem in the first place.

Out of such discussion the clearest proposals to emerge were that high income could be taxed without reducing incentives and production, and that unearned income should be distinguished from earned income for taxation purposes. Unearned income was held to be that which was produced wholly by the operation of social forces rather than the productive effort of individuals. Under this heading might be listed increased property and land values which are not due to any improvement work, profits of invested capital, and inheritance. Taxation on unearned income would not constitute a form of plunder but a claim by society to use, for social purposes, that which it had created. What the New Liberals were putting forward was a positive and constructive role for government fiscal policy. Taxation would not be raised solely to balance the books but for positive programmes of social reform.

The work of Hobhouse and Hobson has been considered here not because they are the only spokesmen for New Liberalism but because they are representative of that school of thought. However, they are not in total agreement and similarities may have been stressed at the expense of differences between them. It does not seem to misrepresent their views in any substantial way to suggest a high degree of consensus on the broad principles outlined above. Social reform is taken as the major theme but this is not to suggest that the anti-imperialism and defence of Free Trade which also characterised New Liberalism were unimportant. It is rather that social reform was the most pressing political issue in the period concerned and in terms of public policy it was here that the New Liberals made a substantial contribution to the debate.

IMPACT ON LEGISLATION

A note of extreme caution must be sounded when looking at the legislative outcomes of New Liberal theory, particularly those acts which constitute the reforms of the Liberal government of 1906–1914. The political and ideological climate of the last two decades of the nineteenth century, and the period up to the outbreak of the First World War, were extremely complex and have generated an extensive literature. The proposals for social reform outlined above were by no means unique to New Liberalism, similar policies being put forward by socialist groups such as the Fabians, by Chamberlainite radicals and by Conservatives. Social reform may not have been a major election issue at any time during this period but the 'condition of England question' exercised the imagination of people of all political persuasions. Many different theses are put forward to explain this intensity of interest, from the growing awareness of the extent of poverty revealed by popular journalism and the statistical investigations of Charles Booth and Seebohm Rowntree, the extension of the franchise, the growth of organised labour and public disturbance by the unemployed, to the desire for 'national efficiency', whether expressed in terms of racial improvement, military efficiency to meet the demands of empire, or both.[23]

Any attempt to reduce the motivation of political actors to single cause explanations, whether this be a desire to further the interests of capital, to secure political advantage over opponents, or to secure the political acquiescence of the working class, will have considerable explanatory weakness. It is not our intention to suggest that the political theory of New Liberalism should displace all or any of the above explanations, since this would be to commit the same error, but to suggest that the understanding of any period in history requires an understanding of the political vocabulary of that period. Only then can some insight be gained into the standards by which some situations were regarded as problems while others were not, and some 'solutions' considered acceptable while others were rejected or not considered at all. It is not intended to imply that philosophers brought about major changes but rather that philosophers provided the basis for understanding the necessity for change.

The political theory of 'New Liberalism' is not claimed as the dominant theory of the age, nor could it even be said to be wholly representative of the Liberal party. The party contained within itself many cross-currents of opinion on the whole range of political issues of the day. Though rejection of tariff reform and the support of Free Trade was a unifying factor, the Liberal party contained both imperialists and anti-imperialists, those in favour of state intervention on social reform and those violently against it, in a bewildering variety of combinations. There were also those, like John Morley, who actively supported many social reform issues but were uncertain as to whether problems were due to causes which would admit to prevention by legislation. It is true that many of the leading figures in the party, notably the future Prime Minister, Asquith, were Oxford men who had come under the influence of Green and Ritchie but the extent of such influences would be impossible to gauge. It is equally true that Lloyd George and Churchill, two of the most vigorous architects of Liberal social legislation, had not been exposed to such influences in their education. What New Liberalism did was to make available a framework for understanding the necessity for change and a set of principles for action within a liberal tradition. Though, like most theories, it did not survive intact the transition from theory to practice, many of its concepts became part of the language of political argument. One means of testing this assertion is to look at some of the principles underlying particular legislation and to attempt to discover a connection with the principles of New Liberalism. To this end we shall examine the Old-Age Pensions Act 1908, the National Insurance Act 1911 and the fiscal policy of the 1909 'People's Budget'.

The debate on old-age pensions had been carried on for a period of thirty years before the Liberal legislation. The participants were drawn from the whole political spectrum and the issue had been the subject of a Royal Commission and five official committees. In spite of some relaxing of the conditions of out-relief, the stigma of pauperism was one which the aged poor who had recourse to the poor law had to bear. Workhouses, which had been intended as a deterrent to the able-bodied, were increasingly the refuge of those no longer capable of work, of which the aged constituted a large proportion. The principle of less eligibility, though applied with varying degrees of severity by different boards of guardians, was applied to a class of persons for whom it was increasingly seen as inappropriate. The 1885 Medical Relief Disqualification Act allowed use of the medical facilities of the poor law without exclusion from the franchise, but the old in receipt of poor relief were still subject to this loss of citizenship rights. Charles Booth had provided statistical evidence of old age as a major cause of poverty, which gave impetus to those who wished to see a shift away from the view that the poverty of the aged was a product of personal failing to its recognition as a social problem with social rather than individual causes. Some form of state pension was seen as the answer to the problem of how the respectable working class might be provided for when their active working lives came to an end. Such a statement, however, conceals the considerable opposition to any form of state pension which held that all distinction between deserving and undeserving would be lost, together with the undermining of the virtues of thrift, self-help, filial responsibility and the instinct for, and exercise of, charity. On the one hand there were those, like Chamberlain, who favoured a contributory insurance scheme as the only solution, on both financial and moral grounds: only thus could a sense of responsibility be ensured. Within this body of opinion there was then disagreement on whether such a scheme should be voluntary or compulsory. On the other hand, there were those, like Booth, who insisted that pensions should be funded solely from taxation since the very poor and many women would be unable to pay contributions. Any contributory scheme would not deal with immediate need since it would take many years to acquire sufficient contributions. Within this body of opinion the disagreement centred around whether such pensions should be universal or restricted and, if the latter, the grounds for such restrictions. Old-age pensions cut across some of the fundamental moral and economic principles of the day.

In 1908 the Liberal government passed the Old-Age Pensions Act which granted non-contributory pensions to persons aged over seventy, subject to certain conditions. Those with incomes of less than £21 p.a. would receive 5s. (25p) weekly, those with incomes of £31 10s. p.a. would receive 1s. (5p) weekly, whereas incomes above this figure disqualified the individual from a pension. Other grounds for disqualification reflect the concern for maintaining the deserving/undeserving distinction. Anyone who had received that category of poor relief which disqualified him as an elector since 1

January 1908, or had failed to work according to his ability, or had been in prison in the previous ten years, was disqualified. Courts would have a discretionary power to disqualify anyone over sixty years of age convicted of drunkenness. These regulations were relaxed in 1911 but it 'was a pension for the very old, the very poor and the very respectable'.[24] The payment was to be completely separate from the Poor Law machinery and receipt would not deprive the pensioner of any civil rights. There is some doubt among historians as to the reasons why the Liberal government introduced the measure at this particular time and the motives behind it. It is not proposed to enter this debate but to indicate some continuity between New Liberal theory and the Act.

Pensions for the aged as of right were a central proposal in New Liberal thought since they were an expression of the organic nature of society. The granting of a pension was a recognition that poverty in old age was a product of social organisation rather than individual failing, and represented a breach in the allocation of reward on purely market criteria. The principle here is one of reward for past services to the community: the duty of the State is to fulfil the obligations of society as a whole to those who have made a contribution to the well-being of society. The method of funding from taxation can also be seen as consistent with the New Liberal demand for redistribution of socially created wealth. Individuals would have a right to a pension so funded because of the contribution made during their working lives to the wealth used to finance the scheme. Pensions can also be viewed as constituting some progress towards the guaranteed minimum standard of life, the basis on which the individual can realise his own good, which was so central to New Liberal thought.

There are, however, some important aspects in which the Act departs from such principles, most notably in the element of selectivity on grounds of income and character. As Hobson insisted, the organic concept of society requires social policy to be of universal benefit and not directed to sectional interests. The element of selectivity, the limitation of benefit to the very poor, required the poor to identify themselves as a separate group and the restrictions made quite severe inroads on the notion of benefit as a right. The character-test element similarly weakened the recognition of the social causes of poverty. Consideration of the amount of pension in terms of principle is more difficult since it could be accounted for purely on financial grounds. The concept of the 'minimum' required for 'self-realisation' is imprecise but an income adequate for subsistence is a fundamental requirement of such a minimum and one which is susceptible to more positive definition. In 1908, 5s. (25p) per week fell below the subsistence minimum of both Booth and Rowntree. It would seem most likely that the figure arrived at was a product both of financial pressure from the Treasury and the need to maintain the principles of thrift and incentive. The Act was inevitably the product of many cross-pressures; the vested interests of Friendly Societies and insurance companies, the demands of organised labour, and a clash of principles between those who supported the Charity Organisation view of poverty and the role of the State and the progressive elements represented by New Liberalism. In spite of the limitations imposed by such pressures the creation of a system of income maintenance separate from the poor law represented a radical break with the principles and practice of the past.

The problems involved in dealing with the aged poor, however, were multiplied and intensified when dealing with two other major problems of the period, personal health and unemployment. Here the Liberal government was dealing with the thorniest of social problems, those experienced by the responsible, able-bodied, adult male who in the past had been considered to be beyond the scope of social assistance by the State. The extent of ill health had been highlighted by the medical functions of the Poor Law and the 1885 Medical Relief Disqualification Act had gone some way towards recognition of the necessity of public provision. The problems were further highlighted by recruitment for the Boer War which revealed the extent of ill health among adult males and prompted the setting-up of a Committee on Physical Deterioration in 1904. The progressive degeneration of the physical health of the working class was a constant theme of the movement for national efficiency. The public health measures of the nineteenth century had concentrated on improving those aspects of the environment which were beyond individual solution and, given a regulated environment, the health of individuals was felt to be a fundamental responsibility of the individual and not of the State.

The problem of unemployment was also present throughout the period under consideration, with periods of trade depression during which it presented itself in severe form. It constituted a primary cause of poverty, a threat to public order and a breeding-ground for socialist organisations. However, tackling the problem of unemployment implied state interference with the organisation of industry and the market. Recognising unemployment as a social rather than an individual problem involved an admission of the imperfections of the system of capitalist production. The detail of the political debates surrounding these issues and the measures taken are well documented. It is proposed here only to look at the principle of insurance through which the Liberals attempted to deal with some of the problems, not only because this illustrates so many of the concerns of New Liberals, but also because insurance remains the basis of social provision in these areas in the modern welfare State.

The National Insurance Act of 1911 was in two parts. Part I, dealing with sickness benefit, provided an income of 10s. (50p) per week and free treatment from a doctor, on the basis of a tripartite contribution of 4d. from employees, 3d. from employers and 2d. from the State. It was to apply to all manual employees between sixteen and seventy years of age and others earning less than £160 per annum. Part II was a provision for unemployment benefit of 7s. (35p) per week (maximum 15 weeks), again on the basis of a tripartite contribution (2½d., 2½d., 1⅓d.) but restricted to certain industries. In both cases the insurance was to be compulsory.

Compulsion appears to be at odds with Liberal theory but it could be justified not only on administrative and actuarial grounds – its efficient working depended on covering both 'good' and 'bad' risks – but also by reference to the New Liberal concept of liberty. If securing the health of the population and protection against the risks of unemployment are understood as benefiting not only the individual but also contributing to the best conditions of the common good then in pursuing these ends the State is fulfilling its function. Without compulsion the objectives of such a scheme would be frustrated since it constitutes a situation 'where action is frustrated if it is not universal, and again where in the absence of regulation one man can directly or indirectly constrain another, infringe his rights, obstruct his rational choice or take advantage of his weakness or ignorance . . . where in the absence of legal control a general desire might be thwarted by individual and perhaps quite selfish objectives'.[25] Compulsory action by the State is thus not restricting liberty but enlarging it, using one form of compulsion to prevent greater infringements of individual liberty. The State provides the conditions under which the individual can contribute to the common good and make the best of himself.

The contributory principle of national insurance can perhaps be interpreted as being at variance with the principles underlying old-age pensions since in insurance the poor are at least partly financing their own benefits, irrespective of their ability to pay. The element of redistribution, demanded by the New Liberal concept of equal opportunity, was minimal. Nevertheless the contributory principle was defended on the grounds that the sharing of responsibility by employees, employers and the State was an expression of the mutual obligation which each owed, and a recognition of the mutual benefit which each derived from the provision. It could thus be seen as embodying the organic nature of society with the responsibility of individuals and society exercised through co-operation. The tripartite contributions performed an important function in moral education.

It was also argued that contributions by employees constituted the firmest basis for providing benefit as a right divorced from the primitive aspects of the Poor Law or the 'conditional' benefits of charity. The Poor Law approach assumed a man to be wholly responsible for his own situation and ignored the social causes of unemployment. To make payments 'conditional' on certain forms of behaviour involved arbitrary decisions on moral worth. Insurance based on contributions could provide an automatic and non-arbitrary basis for benefit; it would depend simply on contributions made and would have an inbuilt mechanism for dealing with persistent idlers. Those who did not work would not pay contributions and would therefore not be eligible for benefit. As Churchill states: 'Our concern is with the evil, not with the causes, with the fact of unemployment, not with the character of the unemployed.'[26] Benefit as a right of citizenship without stigma or discrimination was an essential part of the notion of social provision directed to the good of society as a whole rather than to delinquent minorities. However, the intention did not bear full fruit as all claims for unemployment benefit resulting from personal misbehaviour were to be excluded, perhaps indicating the strength of the notion of deterrence within the Liberal party as a whole.

The Act was a limited measure, falling a long way short, particularly in its unemployment section, of the universal protection outlined by theorists such as Hobhouse and Hobson. It was limited, of course, by many factors: financial constraints, the interests of the medical profession and notions of individual responsibility and the need to exercise voluntary effort over and above state provision, which are as much a part of New Liberal theory as they are of traditional liberalism. The idea of the minimum remained a fairly blunt instrument for operating on the problems of industrial society, particularly when set against the need for individuality and a basic faith in the competitive capitalist system, which new and old liberals alike shared. Theoretically ambiguous, to allow for individual differences, the 'minimum' was a difficult concept to operationalise without interference in the workings of the industrial system on a politically impossible scale. In the case of wages, the government committed itself to the principle of a minimum wage for mining and certain 'sweated trades' but refused to commit itself to specific figures or to extend the principle more generally. National Insurance for sickness and unemployment provided a low basic income and the services of a general practitioner for the insured person (not his family), thus going some way to providing the security which New Liberals saw as encouraging voluntary effort over and above the minimum. The benefits would be both individual and social. The individual would be maintained but at the same time the 'common good' would be furthered by a healthy workforce, increased capacity for consumption and the exercise of personal responsibility which insurance would render more meaningful. The contributory principle not only minimised the amount of market interference but also maintained individual virtues of thrift, the necessary economic incentives and the distinction between deserving and undeserving. It was a mechanism which, though restricted in its initial operation, was capable of extension and that it should have been so extended is perhaps illustrative of the compromise between social and individual responsibility which it represents.

The Liberal government's programme of social reform required substantial changes in fiscal policy to provide the necessary finance. It is perhaps in this area of government policy that we can see the clearest legislative expression of New Liberal ideas. Nineteenth-century views on the principles and purpose of taxation were the subject of a fairly widespread consensus. The orthodox financial position was basically that the purpose of taxation was to 'balance the books' of governments committed to the minimum possible amount of public expenditure. Government should restrict itself to financing activities which the individual could not provide for himself and, in both the provision of services and the raising of finance, there should be as little interference with private activity as possible. Maintenance of the rights of private property took precedence over government activity. The question of who should pay the taxes to be raised and on what basis the amount due was to be calculated was generally answered by the twin principles of 'equality of sacrifice' and 'benefit received'. That is, taxation must make no differentiation between the source or size of income since if governments restricted themselves to provision of public goods the benefits to be derived would accrue to the population as a whole. Any attempt to move towards a progressive system of taxation would be a move towards benefiting one class at the expense of another: one class would bear increased taxation without corresponding increase in benefit. This was objected to both on the grounds of justice and on economic grounds. If the existing distribution of income and wealth reflected the due rewards for initiative and work then any attempt to redistribute through taxation would involve taking the just deserts of one person or class of persons and giving them to those who had no claim to those rewards. Such a procedure not only infringed principles of justice, it would also undermine the whole system of production by weakening the incentive to work, to invest and to accumulate the capital necessary for increasing production capacity. The preference then was always for indirect taxation rather than direct taxation since this maintained equality of sacrifice and ensured that individuals paid some proportion of the cost of the benefit they received.

This view had come under attack from the 1880's onwards by socialists and, as we have seen, by New Liberal theorists. The break with past practice came over a period of years and culminated in the budget of 1909. In 1894 the Liberal government reformed death duties and introduced a degree of progressiveness which constituted a small step towards the recognition of socially-created value to which the State had a claim. In the 1907 budget the principle of differentiation between earned and unearned income was introduced. The full rate of income tax of 1s. (5p) would apply to all unearned income up to £2,000 while earned income would be taxed at the lesser rate of 9d. (4p). Allowances against taxation would only be made against earned income. More importantly, perhaps, Asquith, then the Chancellor, had begun to expand the purpose of the budget: 'The country has reached a stage in which, whether we look merely at its fiscal or its social exigencies, we cannot afford to drift along the stream and treat each year's finance as if it were self-contained. The Chancellor ought to budget, not for one year, but for several years.'[27] Then, in 1909, came Lloyd George's 'People's Budget' which increased land taxes in scope and amount, raised the taxes on unearned income, introduced a supertax on income over £5,000 p.a. and granted a tax allowance of £10 p.a. for every child under sixteen years of age against incomes below £500 p.a. Taking these measures together we can see the connection between them and the New Liberal ideas on property, social value and social reform.

The idea of socially-created value, which denies the absolute right of individual property, runs through all these innovations in fiscal policy. The State has a right to claim a proportion of the income which it has helped to create; the notion of a clearly identifiable social entity with an income of its own is established. Thus death duties, land taxes and taxation of unearned income are all expressions of this right to social income. The redistributive effects of such taxation and the supertax on high incomes reflect the view, outlined by Hobson, that existing distribution of income and wealth may be inefficient, allowing the growth of an unproductive, wasteful surplus. Taxation of such a surplus will therefore not constitute a disincentive, nor will it constitute a simple transfer payment from one class to another. Society as a whole, the 'common good', will benefit by a more efficient use of resources, serving the requirements of economy and justice.

These changes in fiscal policy also reflect the awareness of the interconnected nature of social problems which is so central to the organic concept of society. Old-age poverty, unemployment and sickness cannot be divorced from taxation policy. The budget therefore became an instrument for social reform and social reconstruction, enabling the State to raise an income, in excess of previous expenditure, for positive measures. This was to be considered not only in terms of the present but also for the future, providing for long-term social improvement. It is by reference to New Liberal ideas that we can begin to discern the beginnings of a more comprehensive approach by government to social problems. The Liberal welfare reforms can thus be understood not merely as a set of discrete responses to urgent social and political questions but a move, however tentative, to a continuous and planned policy for social reconstruction. Such a move was a product of many forces over at least three decades and New Liberal theory, though imperfectly realised in practice, played a vital role in the way in which those forces were understood and acted upon. The fact that such ideas did not fully withstand the storm of the First World War and the interwar period does not render them dispensable for a full understanding of the changes in public policy witnessed by the end of the nineteenth century and the beginning of the twentieth.

REFERENCES AND NOTES

1. Freeden, M. (1978) *The New Liberalism*. Oxford University Press, p. 42

2. Green, T. H. (1899) *Prolegomena to Ethics* (ed. A. C. Bradley). Clarendon Press: Oxford, pp. 201–202
3. Green, T. H. (1967) *Lectures on the Principles of Political Obligation*. Longmans: London, para. 7
4. Barker, E. (1928) *Political Thought in England 1848–1914*. Williams and Norgate: London, p. 36
5. Hobhouse, L. T. (1918) *The Metaphysical Theory of the State*. Macmillan: New York, p. 49
6. Ritchie, D. G. (1896) 'Social Evolution', *International Journal of Ethics*, Jan. 1896, p. 166
7. Ritchie, D. G. (1893) *Darwin and Hegel*. Swan Sonnenschein: London, p. 63
8. Hobhouse, L. T. (1898) 'The Ethical Basis of Collectivism', *International Journal of Ethics*, Jan. 1898, p. 145
9. Hobson, J. A. (1974) *The Crisis of Liberalism*. Harvester Press: Brighton, p. 82. First published 1910, P. S. King and Son: London
10. Green, T. H. (1967) para. 223
11. Bosanquet, B. (1892) 'The Principle and Chief Dangers of the Administration of Charity', *International Journal of Ethics* vol. III, p. 323
12. Hobhouse, L. T. (1977) *Liberalism*. Oxford University Press reprint. First published 1911, Williams and Norgate: London, p. 48
13. Hobhouse, L. T. (1922) *Social Evolution and Political Theory*. Columbia University Press: New York, p. 143
14. Hobson, J. A. (1974) p. 164
15. Hobhouse, L. T. (1972) *Democracy and Reaction*. Harvester Press: Brighton, p. 160. First published 1904, T. Fisher Unwin: London
16. Hobson, J. A. (1902) *The Social Problem*. James Nisbet: London, p. 202
17. Hobhouse, L. T. (1977) p. 84
18. Hobhouse, L. T. (1977) p. 83
19. Hobhouse, L. T. (1977) p. 86
20. Hobhouse, L. T. (1922) p. 179
21. Hobson, J. A. (1902) p. 148
22. Hobhouse, L. T. (1977) p. 100
23. See Searle, G. R. (1971) *The Quest for National Efficiency*. Blackwell: Oxford
24. Thane, P. 'Non-Contributory versus Insurance Pension 1878–

1908' in Thane, P. (1978) *The Origin of British Social Policy*. Croom Helm: London, p. 103
25. Hobhouse, L. T. (1922) p. 201
26. W. S. Churchill quoted in Gilbert, B. B. (1966) *The Evolution of National Insurance in Britain*. Michael Joseph: London, p. 272
27. Emy, H. V. (1973) *Liberals, Radicals and Social Politics*. Cambridge University Press: London, p. 200

CONCLUSION

The general picture we have presented is one which depicts the growth of government during the nineteenth century. What was once seen as belonging primarily to the private realm was more and more seen as a proper area for the exercise of government power. From a modest view of government as administering law and keeping order developed a more ambitious view demanding the regulation, reform and improvement of society. However, this development was by no means an even one, and we have tried to show that within each of the major bodies of ideas there were conflicts between those supporting and those resisting the increased power and extent of state action. Both negative and positive attitudes shaped this development and in understanding the century, its thought and its actions, it is important to appreciate the opposing approaches. No general perspective, whether liberal, conservative or socialist, presented a united front either to the problems of the century or to the question of how government should tackle them.

In presenting our picture we have looked at the major political theories of the nineteenth century and their influence on public policy and also at those changes in public policy which clearly affected these ideas. This approach is not the only valid one to describe what happened but we believe that to give a fairly brief general picture an approach which looks at the relationship between ideas and policy is the most fruitful one. In doing this we have looked at the articulate and deliberate presentation of ideas, respecting the views of the participants that their writings could affect public affairs; we have taken seriously their belief that thought and practice should be distinguished but not divorced.

Here, however, a point made throughout this book needs to be once more emphasised and that is the distinction between, on the one hand, the different concepts used by utilitarians, liberals, con-

servatives and socialists, which offered a particular way of understanding reality and thus defined the problems and the possible
solutions and, on the other hand, the values or objectives which
they held which accounted for their preferred aims. Thus even
where the positive suggestions of various writers and thinkers seem
to have had relatively little impact, the concepts which they
adopted, the vocabulary of their political perspectives, guided or
limited, helped or hindered the search for political solutions.

No easy quantification is possible about the relative impact of
ideas; this would be to distinguish too artificially between ideas and
action. Our aim has been to show change as ideas in action, and
thus the story of the nineteenth century, though it can be told in
many ways, is told here as the development of ideas as expressed
both in print and in action. We are aware that more detailed analysis of the events is required stressing the connection between ideas
and practice, in particular case-studies of specific pieces of legislation. Our hope is that the particular approach we have taken will
stimulate more scholarly research into some of the questions which
have been raised. However, if the book serves to introduce the
reader to the major political ideas and the major political changes of
the century and if these two are seen as aspects of the one story
then it will have served its purpose.

BIBLIOGRAPHY

GENERAL READING

The most useful introductory books are:

BEST, G. (1979) *Mid-Victorian Britain 1851–1870*. Fontana: London

BRIGGS, A. (1965) *Victorian People*. Penguin: Harmondsworth; (1955) University of Chicago Press

BRIGGS, A. (1979) *The Age of Improvement 1783–1867*. Longman: London (first published 1959)

CROMWELL, V. (1977) *Revolution or Evolution: British Government in the Nineteenth Century*. Longman: London

EVANS, E. J. (1978) *Social Policy 1830–1914*. Routledge and Kegan Paul: London

FOSTER, J. (1977) *Class Struggle and The Industrial Revolution*. Methuen: London

FRASER, D. (1973) *The Evolution of the British Welfare State*. Macmillan: London

GASH, N. (1979) *Aristocracy and People*. Arnold: London

GRAY, R. (1981) *The Aristocracy of Labour in Nineteenth Century Britain*. Macmillan: London

HENRIQUES, U. R. Q. (1979) *Before the Welfare State*. Longman: London

HOBSBAWM, E. J. (1969) *Industry and Empire*. Penguin: Harmondsworth

HOLLIS, P. (ed.) (1974) *Pressure from Without*. Arnold: London

MACDONAGH, O. (1977) *Early Victorian Government*. Weidenfeld and Nicholson: London

MORRIS, J. (1979) *Pax Britannica* (trilogy). Penguin: Harmondsworth

MUSSON, A. E. (1972) *British Trade Unions 1800–1875*. Macmillan: London

PERKIN, H. (1969) *The Origins of Modern English Society 1780–1880*. Routledge and Kegan Paul: London

READ, D. (1979) *England 1868–1914*. Longman: London

SUTHERLAND, G. (ed.) (1972) *Studies in the Growth of Nineteenth Century Government*. Routledge and Kegan Paul: London

TAYLOR, A. J. (1972) *Laissez-Faire and State Intervention in Nineteenth Century Britain*. Macmillan: London

THOMPSON, E. P. (1968) *The Making of the English Working Class*. Penguin: Harmondsworth

WEBB, R. K. (1980) *Modern England*. George Allen and Unwin: London; Harper and Row: USA

WRIGHT, D. G. (1970) *Democracy and Reform 1815–1885*. Longman: London

There are also two series which are excellent for their treatment of specific topics and for their bibliographical guidance:

Seminar Studies in History (ed. P. Richardson). Longman: London
Studies in Economic and Social History (ed. T. C. Smout). Macmillan: London

INTRODUCTION AND UTILITARIANISM

The best starting point both for a general view of nineteenth-century Britain and for the debate on the influence of ideas on public policy is:

DICEY, A. V. (1905) *Lectures on the Relation Between Law and Public Opinion in England During the Nineteenth Century*. Macmillan: London. Dicey's work is the focus of a great deal of controversy regarding the general role of ideas and the particular influence of Bentham.

The following are a useful introduction to this debate:

BREBNER, J. B. (1948) 'Laissez-Faire and State Intervention in Nineteenth Century Britain', *Journal of Economic History* vol. 8 (supplement)

CLARK, G. KITSON (1959) 'Statesmen in Disguise', *Historical Journal* vol. 2

COATES, W. H. (1950) 'Benthamism, Laissez-Faire and Collectivism', *Journal of the History of Ideas* XI

HART, J. (1965) 'Nineteenth Century Social Reform: A Tory Interpretation of History', *Past and Present* vol. 31

HUME, L. J. (1967) 'Jeremy Bentham and the Nineteenth Century Revolution in Government', *The Historical Journal* vol. 10

MACDONAGH, O. (1958) 'The Nineteenth Century Revolution in Government: A Reappraisal', *The Historical Journal* vol. 1

PARRIS, H. (1960) 'The Nineteenth Century Revolution in Government: A Reappraisal Reappraised', *The Historical Journal* vol. 3

ROBERTS, D. (1959) 'Jeremy Bentham and the Victorian Administrative State', *Victorian Studies* vol. 2

SUTHERLAND, G. (ed.) (1972) *Studies in the Growth of Nineteenth Century Government*. Routledge and Kegan Paul: London. See especially the article by S. E. Finer on Bentham's influence.

For utilitarian thought, the main texts and commentaries are:

BENTHAM, J. (1948) *A Fragment on Government* and *Introduction to the Principles of Morals and Legislation* (ed. W Harrison). Blackwell: Oxford

HALEVY, E. (1952) *The Growth of Philosophical Radicalism*. Faber: London

HAMBURGER, J. (1963) *James Mill and the Art of Revolution*. Yale University Press: New Haven

HUME, L. J. (1981) *Bentham and Bureaucracy*. Cambridge University Press

LIVELY, J. and REES, J. (1978) *Utilitarian Logic and Politics*. Clarendon Press: Oxford

MILL, J. (1955) *Essay on Government* (ed. C. V. Shields). Liberal Arts Press: New York

STEPHEN, L. (1900) *The English Utilitarians* (3 vol). Duckworth: London

STEINTRAGER, J. (1977) *Bentham*. George Allen and Unwin: London

THOMAS, W. (1979) *The Philosophical Radicals*. Clarendon Press: Oxford

For further reading see:

BRIGGS. A. (1959) *The Age of Improvement 1783–1867*. Longman: London

CHECKLAND, S. G. and E. O. (eds) (1974) *The Poor Law Report of 1834*. Penguin: Harmondsworth

CLARK, G. KITSON (1962) *The Making of Victorian England*. Methuen: London

DICKINSON, H. T. (1979) *Liberty and Property.* Methuen: London

FINER, S. E. (1952) *The Life and Times of Sir Edwin Chadwick.* Methuen: London

FINLAYSON, G. B. A. M. (1969) *England in the Eighteen Thirties.* Arnold: London

FRASER, D. (ed.) (1976) *The New Poor Law in the Nineteenth Century.* Macmillan: London

GASH, N. (1979) *Aristocracy and People.* Arnold: London

HENRIQUES, U. R. Q. (1979) *Before the Welfare State.* Longman: London

POYNTER, J. R. (1969) *Society and Pauperism.* Routledge and Kegan Paul: London

SILVER, H. (1975) *English Education and the Radicals 1780–1850.* Routledge and Kegan Paul: London and Boston

LIBERALISM

The most comprehensive guide to the primary sources of nineteenth-century liberalism is:

BRAMSTEAD, E. K. and MELHUISH, K. J. (eds) (1978) *Western Liberalism.* Longman: London.

For more detailed study, the following texts are important:

CHAMBERLAIN, J. (1971) *The Radical Programme* (ed. D. A. Hamer). Harvester Press: Brighton (first published 1885)

MILL, J. S. (1910) *Utilitarianism, On Liberty, Representative Government.* Dent: London; Dutton: New York. (Revised ed. (1972) ed. H. B. Acton)

SPENCER, H. (1969) *The Man versus The State* (ed. D Macrae). Penguin: Harmondsworth (first published 1884)

WARNOCK, M. (ed.) (1962) *Utilitarianism.* Fontana: London

WILLIAMS, G. L. (ed.) (1976) *J. S. Mill on Politics and Society.* Fontana: London

For commentaries on liberalism and its impact on nineteenth-century politics, see the following:

ADELMAN, P. (1970) *Gladstone, Disraeli and Later Victorian Politics.* Longman: London

FEUCHTWANGER, E. J. (1975) *Gladstone.* Allen Lane: London

HAMBURGER, J. (1965) *Intellectuals in Politics*. Yale University Press: New Haven

HAMER, D. A. (1972) *Liberal Politics in the Age of Gladstone and Rosebery*. Clarendon Press: Oxford

HOBHOUSE, L. T. (1977) *Liberalism*. Oxford University Press

MACPHERSON, C. B. (1977) *The Life and Times of Liberal Democracy*. Oxford University Press

READ, D. (1967) *Cobden and Bright: A Victorian Political Partnership*. Arnold: London

ROACH, J. (1957) 'Liberalism and the Victorian Intelligentsia', *Cambridge Historical Journal* vol. XIII no. 1

ROBSON, J. M. (1968) *The Improvement of Mankind*. Routledge and Kegan Paul: London; University of Toronto Press

SOUTHGATE, D. (1962) *The Passing of the Whigs 1832–1886*. Macmillan: London; St Martin's Press: New York

TEN, C. L. (1980) *Mill on Liberty*. Clarendon Press: Oxford

VINCENT, J. (1976) *The Formation of the British Liberal Party 1857–1868* (2nd edition). Harvester Press: Brighton

WATSON, G. (1973) *The English Ideology*. Allen Lane: London

WRIGHT, D. G. (1970) *Democracy and Reform 1815–1885*. Longman: London

CONSERVATISM

The best introductions to conservative thought are:

BUCK, P. W. (ed.) (1975) *How Conservatives Think*. Penguin: Harmondsworth

WHITE, R. J. (ed.) (1964) *The Conservative Tradition* (2nd edition). Black: London

The best introduction to the Conservative party is:

BLAKE, R. (1972) *The Conservative Party from Peel to Churchill*. Fontana: London

For conservative thought, the main texts and commentaries are:

BLAKE, R. (1966) *Disraeli*. Eyre and Spottiswoode: London

BURKE, E. (1975) *On Government, Politics and Society* (ed. B. W. Hill). Fontana: London

COLERIDGE, S. T. (1976) *Collected Works* vol. 10 (ed. J. Colmar).

Routledge and Kegan Paul: London; Princeton University Press: New Jersey

DISRAELI, B. (1913) *Whigs and Whiggism: Political Writings* (ed. W. Hutcheon). Murray: London

FEUCHTWANGER, E. J. (1968) *Disraeli, Democracy and the Tory Party*. Clarendon Press: Oxofrd

FRASER, P. (1966) *Joseph Chamberlain*. Cassell: London

GASH, N. (1953) *Politics in the Age of Peel*. Longman: London

GASH, N. (1965) *Reaction and Reconstruction in English Politics 1832– 1852*. Clarendon Press: Oxford

GREENLEAF, W. H. (1973) 'The Character of Modern Conservatism' in *Knowledge and Belief in Politics* (ed. Benewick, R., Berki, R. N. and Parekh, B.). Allen and Unwin: London

HIMMELFARB, G. (1968) 'Politics and Ideology – The Reform Act of 1867' in her *Victorian Minds*. Weidenfeld and Nicholson: London

MCDOWELL, R. B. (1959) *British Conservatism 1832–1914*. Faber: London; (1974) Greenwood Press: Westport (Conn.)

O'SULLIVAN, N. (1976) *Conservatism*. Dent: London

PINTO DUSCHINSKY, M. (1967) *The Political Thought of Lord Salisbury 1854–1868*. Constable: London

SMITH, F. B. (1966) *The Making of the Second Reform Bill*. Cambridge University Press

SMITH, P. (1967) *Disraelian Conservatism and Social Reform*. Routledge and Kegan Paul: London; University of Toronto Press

SOUTHGATE, D. (1974) *The Conservative Leadership 1832–1932*. Macmillan: London

SOCIALISM

The best general introductions to socialist thought are:

BEER, M. (1953) *A History of British Socialism* vol. I. George Allen and Unwin: London (first published 1919)

COLE, G. D. H. (1953) *Socialist Thought: The Forerunners*. Macmillan: London. One volume in the seven-volume *A History of Socialist Thought*

The main texts and commentaries on socialist thought are:

BERKI, R. N. (1975) *Socialism*. Dent: London

BRIGGS, A. (ed.) (1959) *Chartist Studies*. Macmillan: London

BRIGGS, A. (ed.) (1962) *Fabian Essays*. George Allen and Unwin: London (first published 1889)

BRIGGS, A. and SAVILLE, J. (1971) *Essays in Labour History* vol. 2. Macmillan: London

CHRISTENSEN, T. (1962) *Origin and History of Christian Socialism 1848–1854*. Universitetsforlaget 1: Aarhus

COLE, G. D. H. (1965) *Chartist Portraits*. Macmillan: London; St Martin's Press: New York

COLE, M. (1961) *The Story of Fabian Socialism*. Heinemann: London

HARDIE, J. K. (1974) *From Serfdom to Socialism*. Harvester Press: Brighton (first published 1907)

HARRIS, J. F. (1972) *Unemployment and Politics 1886–1914*. Oxford University Press

HARRISON, R. (1965) *Before the Socialists*. Routledge and Kegan Paul: London; University of Toronto Press

HOBSBAWM, E. J. (1968) *Labouring Men*. Weidenfeld and Nicholson: London

HYNDMAN, H. M. (1973) *England for All : The Text Book of Democracy*. Harvester Press: Brighton (first published 1881, E. W. Allen: London)

MCBRIAR, A. M. (1962) *Fabian Socialism and English Politics 1884–1918*. Cambridge University Press

MACK, M. P. (1955) 'The Fabians and Utilitarianism', *Journal of the History of Ideas* XVI

MATHER, F. C. (1965) *Chartism*. Historical Association Pamphlet G61 (reprinted 1971)

MILIBAND, R. (1954) 'The Politics of Robert Owen', *Journal of the History of Ideas* XV no. 2

MORTON, A. L. (ed.) (1973) *Political Writings of William Morris*. Lawrence and Wishart: London

OWEN, R. (1970) *Report to the County of Lanark and a New View of Society* (ed. V. A. C. Gatrell) Penguin: Harmondsworth (first published 1820)

PAREKH, B. (ed.) (1975) *The Concept of Socialism*. Croom Helm: London

PELLING, H. (1965) *The Origins of the Labour Party*. Clarendon Press: Oxford

PIERSON, S. (1973) *Marxism and The Origins of British Socialism*. Cornell University Press: Ithaca and London

PIERSON, S. (1979) *British Socialists. The Journey from Fantasy to*

Politics. Harvard University Press: Cambridge (Mass.) and London

POLLARD, S. and SALT, J. (eds) (1971) *Robert Owen, Prophet of the Poor.* Macmillan: London

THOMPSON, E. P. (1977) *William Morris: Romantic to Revolutionary.* Merlin Press: London

THOMPSON, L. (1951) *Robert Blatchford.* Victor Gollancz: London

WEBB, B. (1971) *My Apprenticeship.* Penguin: Harmondsworth (first published 1926)

WARD, J. T. (1973) *Chartism.* Batsford: London

WOLFE, W. (1975) *From Radicalism to Socialism 1881–1889.* Yale University Press: New Haven and London

NEW LIBERALISM

The best introductions to New Liberal thought are:

CLARKE, P. (1978) *Liberals and Social Democrats.* Cambridge University Press

FREEDEN, M. (1978) *The New Liberalism.* Oxford University Press

RICHTER, M. (1964) *The Politics of Conscience.* Weidenfeld and Nicholson: London

The main texts and commentaries are:

BRAILSFORD, H. N. (1948) *The Life Work of J. A. Hobson.* L. T. Hobhouse Memorial Trust Lecture Number 17

CLARKE, P. (1978) *Liberals and Social Democrats.* Cambridge University Press

COLLINI, S. (1979) *Liberalism and Sociology. L. T. Hobhouse and Political Argument in England 1880–1914.* Cambridge University Press

COLLINS, D. (1965) 'The Introduction of Old Age Pensions in Great Britain', *The Historical Journal* VIII 2

EMY, H. V. (1973) *Liberals, Radicals and Social Politics.* Cambridge University Press

EVANS, E. J. (ed.) (1978) *Social Policy 1830–1914.* Routledge and Kegan Paul: London

FRASER, D. (1973) *The Evolution of the British Welfare State.* Macmillan: London

FREEDEN, M. (1973) 'J. A. Hobson as a New Liberal theorist: some aspects of his social thought until 1914', *Journal of the History of Ideas* vol. 34

GILBERT, B. B. (1966) *The Evolution of National Insurance in Britain.* Michael Joseph: London

GREEN, T. H. (1889) *Prolegomena to Ethics* (ed. A. C. Bradley). Clarendon Press: Oxford

GREEN, T. H. (1907) *Lectures on the Principles of Political Obligation.* Longman: London

HALLIDAY, J. R. (1971) 'Social Darwinism: A Definition', *Victorian Studies* vol. 14 no. 4

HARRIS, J. F. (1972) *Unemployment and Politics 1886–1914.* Oxford University Press

HAY, J. R. (1975) *The Origins of the Liberal Welfare Reforms 1906–1914.* Macmillan: London

HOBHOUSE, L. T. (1898) 'The Ethical Basis of Collectivism', *International Journal of Ethics* vol. 8

HOBHOUSE, L. T. (1911) *Liberalism.* Williams and Norgate: London

HOBHOUSE, L. T. (1918) *The Metaphysical Theory of the State.* Macmillan: London

HOBHOUSE, L. T. (1922) *Social Evolution and Political Theory.* Columbia University Press: New York

HOBSON, J. A. (1902) *The Social Problem.* James Nisbet: London

HOBSON, J. A. (1974) *The Crisis of Liberalism.* Harvester Press: Brighton (first published 1910)

HOBSON, J. A. (1976) *Confessions of an Economic Heretic.* Harvester Press: Brighton

LYND, H. M. (1945) *England in the 1880s: Towards a Social Basis for Freedom.* Oxford University Press

NICHOLLS, D. (1962) 'Positive Liberty 1880–1914', *American Political Science Review* (March)

OWEN, J. T. (1974) *L. T. Hobhouse, Sociologist.* Thames Nelson: London

RITCHIE, D. G. (1891) *Principles of State Interference.* Swan Sonnenschein: London

RITCHIE, D. G. (1909) *Darwinism and Politics.* Swan Sonnenschein: London

ROGERS, J. A. (1972) 'Darwinism and Social Darwinism', *Journal of the History of Ideas* vol. 33

SIDGWICK, H. (1902) *Lectures on the Ethics of T. H. Green, Mr Herbert Spencer and Mr. Martineau.* Macmillan: London

THANE, P. (ed.) (1978) *The Origins of British Social Policy.* Croom Helm: London

NINETEENTH-CENTURY PERIODICALS

Though we have tried, as far as possible, to refer to readily available texts in outlining the political thought of the nineteenth century, much of the controversy and many of the debates are to be
found in the journals of the period. The ones which we found most
valuable are listed below with some brief comments, together with
a slightly longer list of journals which also proved useful.

Edinburgh Review: founded in 1802, edited briefly by Sydney
Smith and then, for a quarter of a century, by Francis Jeffrey. It
represented the reforming Whig approach to politics, later becoming more conservative, but it opened its pages to a variety of radical
and reforming writers.

Quarterly Review: founded in 1809, representing the Tory
approach.

Westminster Review: founded in 1824 to represent the Benthamite
school. Both the Mills were regular contributors until 1828. In 1835
the philosophical radicals founded the *London Review* and in the
following year the two reviews merged into the *London and Westminster*; in 1840 the title reverted to the *Westminster Review*.

Saturday Review: founded in 1855 as an outlet for the Peelites, it
remained independent of the two parties and stood for moderate
conservatism.

Fortnightly Review: founded in 1865 and edited from 1867–83 by
John Morley, it was the major forum for liberal debate.

Also useful (with dates of their establishment):

Bentley's Quarterly Review (1859)
Blackwood's Edinburgh Magazine (1817)
British Quarterly Review (1845)
Contemporary Review (1866)
Cornhill Magazine (1860)
Fraser's Magazine (1830) became *Longman's Magazine* (1882)
London Magazine (1820)
National Review (1855) revived (1883)
Nineteenth Century (1877)

INDEX